UNCOMMON WOMEN

UNMARKED TRAILS

Also By Suzanne Schrems

Across The Political Spectrum: Oklahoma Women In Politics In
The Early Twentieth Century

UNCOMMON WOMEN
UNMARKED TRAILS

The Courageous Journey Of
Catholic Missionary Sisters In
Frontier Montana

Suzanne H. Schrems, Ph.D.

Horse Creek Publications, Inc.
Norman, Oklahoma

Uncommon Women, Unmarked Trails
Copyright (c) 2003 Horse Creek Publications, Inc.
First Printing 2003
Manufactured in the United States of America

Cover design: Edward L. Schrems, Norman, Oklahoma
Front Cover Picture: Sisters of Providence at St. Ignatius Mission. Courtesy of Sisters of Providence, Seattle.
Back cover photo: Edward L. Schrems, Norman, Oklahoma

Publisher's Cataloging in Publication
(Provided by Quality Books, Inc.)

Schrems, Suzanne H.
    Uncommon women, unmarked trails : the courageous journey of Catholic missionary sisters in frontier Montana / Suzanne H. Schrems. -- 1st ed.
    p. cm.
    Includes bibliographical references and index.
    LCCN 2002108126
    ISBN 0-9722217-0-0

    1. Ursulines--Missions--Montana. 2. Sisters of Charity of Providence--Missions--Montana. 3. Missions--Montana.
4. Indians of North America--Missions--Montana. 5. Montana--History. I. Title.

BV2803.M9S37 2003   266'.2'786
                              QBI02-200740

CONTENTS

PREFACE

I visited with the Ursuline Nuns at their convent in Brown County, Ohio, just east of Cincinnati, in 1978. The sisters invited me to stay for lunch, and it was during our luncheon conversation that they proudly mentioned the nineteenth-century Ursulines who volunteered as missionaries to educate Native Americans in Montana. I thought this to be an interesting piece of trivia and tucked it away in memory. I did not recall it until many years later when I was researching the role of women in the development of the American West. My research, however, revealed very little on the work of the Catholic sisters. I did discover in reading about Catholic missions in the Northwest that the Jesuit fathers dominated the literature. Even though the Jesuits relied on women religious to perform numerous educational and domestic functions at their missions, their numerous histories included little concerning the Catholic sisters' labors in educating and converting Native Americans. The study that follows, therefore, contributes to the religious history of the American West by including the role of Catholic sisters in the education and acculturation of Native American children.

My initial search for sources relating to the Ursulines' work in Montana revealed the history of the Sisters of Charity of Providence who, in 1864, were the first sisters to establish Indian mission schools in Montana. Although there were Catholic sisters from several orders working in Montana in the nineteenth century, this study focuses on the Ursuline

Nuns and Sisters of Providence because they were the first to establish schools at Jesuit missions and the first women in Montana to work with Native American children.

I am indebted to archivists at convents across the country who have generously given of their time to provide me with letters and manuscripts of the pioneer sisters who volunteered for missionary service in Montana. I am especially grateful to Sister Mary Rose Krupp, archivist at the Ursuline Convent in Toledo, Ohio, and Sister Elizabeth Kramer, archivist at the School Sisters of Saint Francis in Milwaukee, Wisconsin. Sister Therese Dufrefse, secretary general of Providence Mother House in Montreal, provided me with what little information is available concerning the sisters who went to St. Ignatius Mission in 1864. Sister Dufrefse is very busy, and I appreciate her time on my behalf. I also appreciate the kindness and guidance of Brother Edward Jennings, S.J., at the Jesuit Archives, Foley Library, Gonzaga University, Spokane, Washington.

Researching Catholic sisters in Montana from the Plains of Oklahoma is difficult. Carolyn Mahin, with interlibrary loan at the University of Oklahoma, eased this difficulty. Carolyn's expertise and persistence helped me to acquire many worthwhile materials.

Uncommon Women
Unmarked Trails

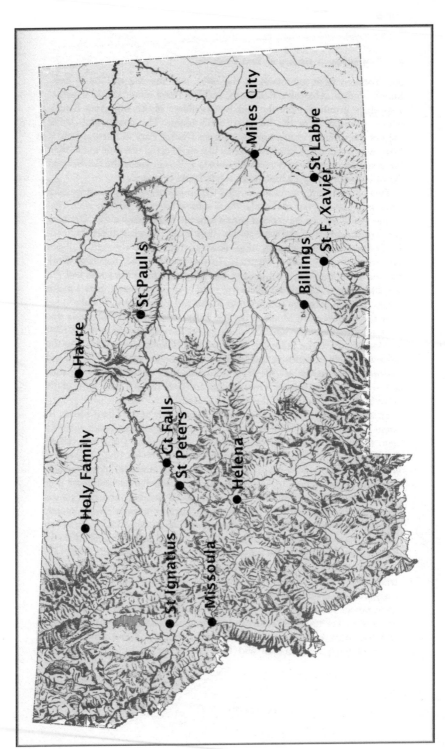

Map of Montana based on USGS physical map. (Towns and missions added by publisher.)

1

UNCOMMON WOMEN

After attending early Mass on a dark cold November morning in 1856, Mother Joseph and four of her sisters from the Sisters of Providence convent in Montreal, Canada, hurriedly ate their breakfast and rushed to catch the train leaving for New York City. Once in New York, they anxiously awaited the departure of the *S.S. Illinois*, a departure delayed until the captain learned of the winner of the United States presidential election. Once the captain had this information to take to settlers on the West Coast, he directed his ship out of New York Harbor destined for the Isthmus of Panama. On November 17th, the sisters departed the ship in Panama and traveled by mule across the Isthmus to the Pacific Coast, where they boarded the *Golden Age* to continue their journey to the Northwest. On December 3rd, the sisters landed in San Francisco and left again two days later aboard the *Brother Jonathan*. They arrived at their destination at Fort Vancouver, Washington Territory, on the ninth of December. Mother Joseph of the Sacred Heart, Mother Superior of this newly established Sisters of Providence Foundation at Fort Vancouver, made the trip from Vancouver to Montreal and back many times during the initial stages of community building, in the Pacific Northwest. The sisters she escorted to their new foundation established schools and hospitals, which provided needed services to the growing population of settlers that immigrated to the Northwest throughout the latter half of the nineteenth century. But perhaps the most challenging of assignments for the Sisters of Providence was to build and administer schools and hospitals for Native Americans at Indian missions in Montana.

Twenty years later, in 1884, Mother Amadeus and five Ursuline nuns from Toledo, Ohio, disembarked from the Northern Pacific Railroad in Miles City, Montana. Their destination was the Cheyenne Reservation, where they intended to establish a school at St. Labre's Mission. Between 1884 and 1900, the Ursulines established six schools for Native American children on reservations through out eastern Montana.

The Sisters of Providence and the Ursuline nuns pioneered women's missionary activities among the Flathead, Blackfoot, Crow, Cheyenne, and Gros Ventre-Assiniboine Indians. They were nineteenth-century women from America and Canada who made a conscious decision to lead a life uncommon to most women of the time. They traded marriage and family for a religious environment that offered opportunities to engage in work they believed would reward them eternally by bringing the children and the needy to God's love.

Generally, women in the nineteenth century found limited opportunities to advance themselves personally or professionally. Society did not afford them the same educational opportunities as men to prepare them to become self-sufficient and independent. Education was gender-based, reinforcing society's perception of men's and women's separate roles. Women's place was the domestic realm of the home where it was their duty to uphold the virtues and moral character of society and to provide for their families a peaceful sanctuary from the chaotic work world of industrial America.

Women's moral obligation to guide mankind fortuitously opened opportunities for them as teachers, missionaries, and reformers. In these fields of usefulness, women enjoyed professional recognition, realized personal fulfillment, and found economic security. Once married, however, their opportunities diminished. They often found it difficult to combine the duties of wife and mother with professional responsibilities; their place in the home took precedence over outside concerns. A woman, if she remained single, was more likely to accomplish personal and professional goals. But, society viewed single women negatively, often labeling them old maids. There was pressure for women to marry early to avoid being stigmatized as crones who were "stiff, unbending, soured, and jealous." Women could escape society's domestic prescription, however, by joining religious communities and making a professed commitment to God and a religious life. Convents offered some women an acceptable alternative to marriage, wherein they might receive an education, economic independence, and professional opportunities. As members of a congregation, sisters worked together to establish schools, orphanages, hospitals, and charitable agencies, where they found both useful work and personal satisfaction.

Women's entrance into religious life coincided with the founding of new female religious congregations in America and Canada in the nineteenth century. In America, the increase in Catholic immigrants from heavily Catholic European countries such as Ireland and Germany caused overcrowding of church- related institutions. To meet the needs of the growing Catholic population, bishops appealed to superiors of European convents to establish branches of their foundations in the United States. Between 1830 and 1859, Catholic sisters established thirty-nine new congregations.

In Canada, where the Sisters of Providence established their first convent, the increase in women's religious communities paralleled the growth in power and influence of the Catholic church. The Church assumed a powerful political role in society by its active opposition to unification of French and English Canadians and by its role in solving developing social problems in big cities. Church involvement in providing social services created a need for new women's religious foundations to establish schools and social agencies. The Ursuline Nuns and Sisters of Providence established branches of their foundations in North America during this period of Catholic institution-building. In 1849, Bishop Rappe of Cleveland requested that the Ursuline Congregation of Paris in Boulogne-sur-mer send sisters to establish a branch of their community in northern Ohio. The original intent of the Ursuline foundation in Europe, from its inception in 1535 to the early 1600s, was to care for diseased and homeless people. By 1612, the focus of the foundation changed from community involvement to an enclosed society where the sisters provided education for young girls in convent boarding schools.

Emily Travernier Gamelin founded the Sisters of Charity of Providence in Montreal in 1843. The order grew out of Madame Gamelin's concern for the condition of homeless aged women who needed shelter, medical care, and counseling. With limited financial resources left by her late husband, Madame Gamelin started a home for women that provided beds, food, and medical assistance. The increase in women needing shelter caused Madame Gamelin to seek funding from wealthy individuals, who were ultimately instrumental in the construction of a large two-story boarding house. It was difficult for Madame Gamelin and the charitable ladies who assisted her to provide the spiritual and physical guidance required to maintain the women's shelter. Bishop Bourget of Montreal requested that the Sisters of Charity of St. Vincent de Paul in France take over the work initiated by Madame Gamelin. The superior general of the French order could not spare any of her sisters and turned down the bishop's request. Bishop Bourget, determined to see that the charitable work of Madame Gamelin and her friends continue, founded a diocesan community similar to the Sisters of Charity. He called for volunteers to be trained in the religious life. Seven women, including Madame Gamelin, volunteered. After several months of religious instruction, they took their vows and became the first Sisters of Charity of Providence, more commonly known as the Sisters of Providence. The concern of the order was to provide education, medical care, counseling, homes, and hospitals for the disadvantaged.

At the same time that women's religious congregations were expanding in eastern Canada and the United States, Protestant and Catholic missionary societies began sending missionaries to the American West. Bringing Christianity to the people of the Rocky Mountains and the Pacific Northwest began in 1834 when Protestant missionaries Jason and Daniel Lee built their mission on the banks of the Willamette River. A year later, two French Canadians employed by the Hudson's Bay Company petitioned Monsignor Provencher of St. Boniface, Manitoba, for priests to minister to Catholics residing in Oregon Country. In response to this request, the Monsignor sent Father Norbet Blanchet and Father Modeste Demers from Montreal in 1838. They established the first Roman Catholic church in the Pacific Northwest on the Cowlitz River north of Fort Vancouver. Two years later Pierre Jean De Smet, a Jesuit missionary from Belgium, arrived in the region to investigate the possibility of organizing a mission field to convert and acculturate Native Americans. Encouraged by his reception and the willingness of Native Americans to receive religious instruction, De Smet traveled to Europe to recruit Jesuit missionaries to help establish Indian missions. De Smet and his followers ultimately developed two dozen missions, where they struggled to change Indian culture with an inculcation of European practices and beliefs.

Once the Jesuits established Indian missions in the Pacific Northwest and Rocky Mountains, they needed the help of Catholic sisters to build and staff mission schools. The sisters were eager to volunteer as missionaries because they believed that guiding the Indian soul to heaven was serving God in the most worthy manner. Those who chronicled the experiences of western missionary sisters often described their adventures in the West as "woman's part in the winning of souls for Christ." Life at western missions also provided the harsh, deprived life of a good religious. One sister wrote that the sisters "pledged themselves to tread the hard and narrow way," and that the sisters "undertook the pioneer's rigorous life of privation." Besides altruistic goals, missionary life offered women the opportunity to test their faith and their ability to live without worldly comforts. On reservations in Montana, the Sisters of Providence and the Ursuline Nuns experienced hardship, sacrifice, and poverty, all requirements for leading an exemplary life.

In the austere mission environment, the sisters worked to bring Catholic Christianity and European standards of civilization to Native American children. At mission boarding schools, the sisters taught Native American girls domestic skills so that as wives and mothers they could assume their proper role in Victorian society. Teaching the art of homemaking, however, was a difficult task for women who chose not to live in domesticity. Both the Sisters of Providence and Ursuline Nuns received an education that emphasized academic over domestic skills. For example, the women who joined the Ursuline Congregation in Ohio generally came from middle-to upper-class families. As young girls, most started their education in convent boarding and day schools. As members of the Ursuline Order, they continued their academic training with college courses in history, science, math, French and German, grammar, philosophy, and music.

The Sisters of Providence also received academic training that enabled them to care for the sick and needy. There is little information concerning the educational background of these sisters. Available sources indicate, however, that in Montreal they worked to provide medical assistance for underprivileged and destitute people. The medical faculty at the University of Victoria trained the sisters in diagnostic techniques and pharmacology. At St. Ignatius Mission in Montana, the sisters not only taught domestic arts, but also expanded their responsibilities to include caring for the sick in the convent and in the homes of Native Americans on the reservation.

It was the sisters' responsibility at Jesuit missions to develop and operate their institutions. This responsibility, one they likely would not have experienced in their eastern convents, challenged the sisters' obedience to congregational rule as set forth in their constitutions. The constitutions of women's religious communities stated the purpose of the congregation, the role of the sisters in fulfilling the community's goals, and how the community would be governed. As extensions of European foundations, American communities tried to follow the European rule of enclosed, contemplative communities where sisters devoted their time to prayer.

In 1884, when the Ursuline Nuns arrived in Montana from Toledo, they still practiced enclosure. The sisters, however, found it difficult to uphold the discipline of their religious life in the frontier environment. At western missions, they could not always follow the routine and ritual of congregational life as they practiced it in their eastern convents. To accomplish their missionary goals, the Ursulines worked outside the rule of their order to acquire the necessary financial resources and materials to build convents and schools at each Jesuit mission. Unlike the Ursuline Nuns, the Sisters of Providence did not practice the rule of enclosure. This, perhaps, allowed them more freedom to pursue their missionary work.

The Montana sisters found it necessary to adapt their religious culture to accommodate frontier conditions and mission life. Cultural adaptation was a common experience shared by many women who emigrated to the West in the nineteenth century. The sisters, like many western women, modified certain aspects of their culture in order to be successful in building religious institutions and working with Native Americans. In so doing, however, the sisters, as women of God, could operate under a different set of rules than most western women. For one, the cloak of religiosity that surrounded the sisters provided for them an acceptable cover under which to engage in activities that were usually part of men's role-- obtaining financial support to establish and maintain their institutions. At all missions, the sisters sought innovative ways in which to secure enough money to build convents, hospitals, and mission schools.

The sisters also were able to work around the prevailing attitude in the nineteenth century that male members of society were the final authority on most issues, even those concerning women. Typically, whether in diocesan or mission communities, Catholic sisters were under the authority of male clerics of the Catholic church. Women religious, however, enjoyed a certain amount of autonomy from Church authority because bishops and clerics needed the sisters' labors to support Church-related institutions. In Montana the sisters were under the authority of Jesuit priests. The Jesuits could not educate Native American children without the assistance of the sisters. Because of this, the sisters could negotiate their terms and demands and thus assume some control over their affairs. Their final bargaining tool was the threat of withdrawal from the mission. When conflicts occurred at Jesuit missions in Montana, the sisters always maintained control of their institutions and the integrity of their orders.

Finally, the Catholic sisters' experiences were different than most western women because the sisters did not work within the structure of normal domestic roles. Unencumbered by the responsibilities of husband, home, and family, the sisters were more independent in their affairs and could devote themselves to the accomplishment of personal and professional goals. But, the frontier environment presented challenges for all women; and, like other women, the sisters found new strengths and abilities in response to frontier life. Often, unpredicted hardships forced these uncommon women to find within themselves the courage, the endurance, and the will to continue their work, and perhaps most importantly, the humor to ease difficult situations as they journeyed down unmarked trails to realize their goals to bring Christianity and civilization to the inhabitants of the frontier West.

St. Ignatius Mission c. 1880's. Courtesy of Jesuit Oregon Province Archives, Gonzaga University, Spokane.

2

THE TRAIL TO
ST IGNATIUS

In June, 1864, Mother Joseph once again traveled from Vancouver
to Montreal and from there she escorted five sisters back to the Vancouver
convent. The sisters followed the same route as those who had preceded
them. But their journey did not end in Vancouver. Their final destination
at St. Ignatius Mission in Montana was another 550 miles inland. On September
12th, Sister Mary of the Infant Jesus, Sister Mary Edouard, and
Sister Remi, accompanied by three Jesuit Fathers, traveled by covered
wagon to the Providence foundation at Walla Walla along the Columbia
River in present day Washington State. The sisters rested at Walla Walla
while they prepared for their journey over the mountains. In particular,
their garments had to be altered so as to accommodate travel by horseback
and to protect them from cold and rain. On the backs of their horses they
carried their bedrolls and carpetbags, which also served as pillows when
they camped at night. Sister Paul Miki joined the Montreal sisters when
they left Walla Walla for the trek over the mountains to St. Ignatius Mission
on the Flathead Reservation in what is now western Montana. They
traveled first by horseback for twelve days through unmarked wilderness
to Lake Coeur d' Alene in present-day Idaho. Each night of their journey,
they set up their camp, bedded down, and rehashed the day's events. One
sister wrote, "At night we enjoyed a rest sweetened by prayer, the singing
of hymns and the best meal that anyone could wish for in the desert. Alone
in our tent, we four chatted freely, according to our program, reminding

one another of and laughing at the few amusing things that had occurred during the day." After a week's layover at Lake Coeur d'Alene, the sisters crossed the lake in flatboats and continued on horseback to Sacred Heart Mission in present day Idaho. A family from the Flathead Reservation met the sisters at Sacred Heart and escorted them over the Coeur d'Alene Mountains to the Flathead Valley. The sisters arrived at their new home among the Flatheads on October 17, four months after leaving Montreal. The sisters' trip marked many firsts, not only for the Sisters of Providence, but also for western women in general. The four were the first white women to cross the Rocky Mountains, and the first women to build institutions in present day Montana to bring "civilization" and Christianity to western inhabitants.

Shortly after the sisters arrived at St. Ignatius in October, 1864, Mother Joseph thought it prudent to write Father Grassi, Jesuit Superior of the Flathead Mission, to ask for his patience in working with the new recruits from Montreal. She informed Fr. Grassi that, "Of the four nuns who are now missionaries at your place, three are young, in age and in religion. Evidently, they will require indulgence especially on your part." Sister Mary of the Infant Jesus, Superior of the Montana congregation, was the most mature of the sisters at St. Ignatius. When she arrived at the mission, she was thirty-eight years old and had been a member of the Sisters of Providence for fourteen years. Mother Joseph, however, worried about the Montana superior's inexperience. She explained to Father Grassi that "Sister Superior relies greatly on your experience for help and advice in the direction of her sisters and of her house. She is well aware of her insufficiency; still, she appears to us to be animated by good will and the desire of devoting herself."

Mother Joseph believed that she needed to express her concerns to Father Grassi about the sisters' welfare and their success in establishing a school at St. Ignatius. The mother superior feared that without Jesuit assistance the sisters would most likely find mission life too difficult, and the challenges of establishing a convent and school insurmountable. The Jesuit fathers offered to help the sisters by providing limited financial and material aid. The assistance offered, however, placed the women in a dependent situation that interfered with the sisters' efforts to build their own religious institutions at the mission. One of the problems, then, confronting the sisters at St. Ignatius, was how to work successfully with the Jesuits toward the mutual goal of Native American acculturation, while maintaining their independence and upholding the integrity of their order. But perhaps a bigger obstacle to the sisters' success was the language and cultural barriers between them and the Native Americans on the reservation. Until the Sisters of Providence could demonstrate to Native American parents the merits of their school, they found it difficult to implement religious and educational programs that would assimilate Native American children into the mainstream of American culture.

The Jesuit fathers initially established St. Ignatius Mission on the Pend d' Oreille River near the Washington-Idaho border in 1854. The mission at that location was not a success. Spring floods washed cultivated soil and seed downstream, causing food shortages and near- starvation. A Kalispel chief suggested that the missionaries move the mission east of the mountains to a valley that was a favorite gathering spot of interior bands of Kalispel, Kutenai, and Flatheads. Finding the chief's suggested site favorable for mission activities, the Jesuits reestablished St. Ignatius Mission in the Flathead Valley in present-day western Montana.

In 1855, Governor Isaac I. Stevens, of Washington Territory, negotiated a treaty with the Flathead, Pend d' Oreille, and the Kutenai people, according to which they agreed to cede their lands and accept joint occupancy of a 1,280,000 acre reservation near St. Ignatius Mission. The treaty stipulated that the federal government would allocate funds for improvements on the reservation and provide a hospital and school for the education of Indian children. The federal government gave the Jesuits the authority to carry out these stipulations. Accordingly, they started a school for boys in 1856. The missionaries, however, did not receive the promised funds and subsequently closed the school.

The Jesuits continued to maintain the mission and provide religious instruction. They also initiated internal improvements that made the mission self-sufficient. By 1863, the priests were ready to develop a program to educate Indian boys to become industrious farmers and good Catholics. They also believed it important to provide religious instruction for Native American girls and to educate them in domestic arts so that they would make acceptable wives and mothers for Native boys. The Jesuits believed that Catholic sisters could provide the best environment in which to teach Native American girls civilized habits and Christian piety.

Sisters of Providence first convent. St. Ignatius Mission, 1864. Courtesy of
Sisters of Providence, Seattle.

Mother Mary of the Infant Jesus with two Flathead women. St. Ignatius
Mission. Courtesy of Sisters of Providence, Seattle.

The sisters' first convent and boarding school at St. Ignatius was a small log cabin built by the Jesuit fathers, who constructed similar cabins for Native Americans on the reservation. The sisters' cabin, or Holy Family School, consisted of four rooms including a kitchen and a ten- square-foot dormitory loft. Their primitive cabin had few amenities. They could order necessary goods from St. Louis, Missouri, but it took over a year for them to arrive in western Montana. It was especially difficult to prepare meals. Until supplies arrived from St. Louis, the sisters cooked over an open fire without the benefit of a frying pan, and only had twelve goblets to use as their dinnerware.

Acquiring financial resources to operate and expand their convent and school was very difficult for the sisters in their first years at St. Ignatius. Typically, religious orders relied on tuition from students to support their educational institutions. Missionaries who established schools on reservations, however, relied on the United States government to help financially with the education of Native American children. After the ratification of the Stevens Treaty in 1859, agents to the Flathead Reservation had a difficult time acquiring promised government annuities for the support of reservation families, including funds for a school and hospital. In 1860, the government sent the Flatheads $25,000 of spoiled goods that were of little use. In 1864, the government allocated $1,800 toward the education of Native American children at St. Ignatius. Thereafter, government aid was withheld until 1874.

Without federal funds, the sisters could not proceed with their missionary program or exercise their autonomy at the mission. Instead they had to rely on the Jesuits for "our food as well as board and room for the pupils and patients." In payment the sisters became responsible for the care of the Church, milkhouse, bakery, and laundry, including ironing, mending, and sewing for the fathers. A certain amount of friction developed between the two religious orders over the work the Jesuits assigned to the sisters. The sisters maintained the domestic chores that they performed for the fathers were not a part of the original agreement between the sisters and Father Giorda. Father Joseph Giorda, Superior of the Rocky Mountain Missions, had completed an agreement with the sisters that stipulated the responsibilities of the sisters and the Jesuits at the mission. The agreement stated that the fathers would give the sisters government appropriations for schools, but that they were not responsible if the government did not pay the money. The agreement also stated that they would provide the sisters with flour, meat, vegetables, coffee, tea, and sugar for as long as the women could not support themselves. The sisters' part of the agreement stated that they would keep a day school for Native American boys and girls, would take care of the sick in their lodges, would see to the up keep of the Church, and would start a boarding school for young white girls.

The sisters believed that to uphold the mandate of their order, which stipulated their responsibility to provide for the needy, they had to become financially independent of the Jesuit fathers. There were, however, few opportunities available for the sisters to acquire the necessary funds to support their convent and school. A lack of funds also hampered the charitable work of the Sisters of Providence at the Motherhouse in Vancouver. The Vancouver sisters solved their financial dilemma by resorting to one of the only options available to them--traveling to the goldmining regions to beg among the miners. The St. Ignatius sisters considered begging "repugnant to nature and humiliating," but necessary if they were to accomplish their goals. Because the Vancouver sisters claimed jurisdiction over begging operations in the Vancouver and Walla Walla area, the sisters from St. Ignatius had to travel great distances to mining camps in central Montana to solicit funds. These trips were often difficult and dangerous for the sisters. They did not generally fear for their safety when on their own in the wilderness. But when they stayed at roadhouses along the route to the mines, they sensed a certain element of danger. At one roadhouse, an unknown person, foreseeing that the sisters might need assistance, placed a pistol under their pillow for protection.

Between 1867 and 1872, the sisters collected $9,300 from their annual begging tours. They turned this money over to the Jesuits in payment for support of their convent and school. This final payment ended the initial contract between the sisters and the Jesuits. The sisters were now independent and not under any obligation to work for the Jesuit fathers. Mother Caron, General Superior of the Sisters of Providence (1872-1878), who was visiting the sisters' foundations in the West, arrived at St. Ignatius in time to negotiate a new contract between the sisters and Jesuits. The contract, dated November 4, 1872, stipulated that the Jesuit fathers would sell to the Sisters of Providence "buildings by them occupied, with furniture, and with a lot of ground on which the buildings stand, with the exception of the baking house and the milk house with their respective implements." The agreement also stated that the sisters would accept the responsibility of the school and charge of the sacristy. In return, the fathers would provide them with five hundred pounds of beef and one thousand pounds of flour each year. The fathers also agreed to turn over all government money for schools to the sisters.

Until the sisters could build a boarding school for reservation children, their log cabin convent became a temporary shelter. It took awhile, however, for Native American families to understand that the missionaries expected the parents to place their children in the sisters' care. While the sisters waited for reservation children to enroll at their school, they accepted boarders from the near by community. This turned out to be a very favorable arrangement. The first boarders were two Metis girls and a Pend d' Oreille woman and her two children. The woman, Sabine, was adept at hunting, and helped the sisters by supplying deer meat, berries, and native foods. But perhaps more importantly, she spoke French as well as Salish, and served as an interpreter for the sisters who spoke only French.

The fact that the sisters could speak only French concerned Native American parents. Salish was the common language spoken by the Flathead, Pend d' Oreille, and Kutenai people on the reservation, and they expected the missionaries to speak Salish as well. One chief berated the sisters by telling them "If you can't learn the Indian language, go back to Montreal. You are no good to us here." The Jesuits were quick to realize that before the sisters could provide instruction to Native American girls, they needed to learn Salish. Shortly after they arrived at the mission, Father Grassi met with the sisters to teach the prayers of the Catechism in Salish. After a few months, the sisters had learned some prayers and could communicate a few Salish words.

In 1865, the sisters enrolled nine girls from the reservation at the boarding school. Native American parents, however, were still apprehensive about the sisters' school. Sister Mary of the Infant Jesus commented that :

> As soon as they were clothed and clean the parents withdrew them. Also, far from being grateful for this care of their children, and without paying for their board and keep, they invented malicious remarks about us and our house ... some went as far as to say their children had been

infested with lice ... that we had confiscated their things
and that we beat the children with sticks....

The remarks were believed by the parents who did not really know
what sisters were. Perhaps the parents were reluctant to allow the missionaries to educate their children to the ways of white culture, which had little
relevance in Native American life. The missionaries placed great emphasis
on the importance of educating girls in the culture of nineteenth-century
white women. The sisters' educational programs taught Native American
girls the virtues of Victorian womanhood and the necessary economic
skills needed to be "helpmates" in white culture.

The Jesuits believed that the sisters, by their very presence, would
provide living examples of the virtues and character of refined womanhood. It delighted the priests when the sisters began to demonstrate these
virtues shortly after their arrival. One father wrote:

> They scarcely set foot inside their temporary quarters,
> when they were already engaged in educational work of
> various kinds; that is, sweeping, cleaning, washing, and
> scrubbing. These were the first object lessons given by
> those valiant women to the crowd of Indians, who stood
> around in open-eyed wonderment.

The missionaries had little understanding of Native American culture or the important economic role of women in Native American society.
Before white contact, Native American parents taught their daughters
to perform economic activities; the survival of Native American culture
relied on women's economic contribution. The Flatheads began teaching
their children to assume adult responsibilities in their pubescent years.
For girls, education coincided with menarche. At the onset of a girl's first
menses, her mother appointed a wise old woman of the tribe to act as the
girl's guardian and instructor. The mother was selective in her choice of a
guardian. It was important that she select a women who displayed qualities
of chastity and industry and possessed sufficient skills. Girls lived in their
guardians' lodges for four days while they were being instructed on virtues of life that included sobriety, industry, frugality, and obedience. There
was also instruction on the value of hard work. During this initial learning

period, a young girl supplied four loads of firewood each morning and evening for the camp and replenished the water supply. She was expected to make all the meals for her family without assistance from others and could not eat any of the food herself. This was also the time in a girl's life when her mother, guardian, and other women of the tribe instructed her in the arts of woman's work. From the beginning of puberty until marriage, girls prepared food, cured meats, tanned hides, and made clothing. These skills were important to the tribe's economic survival and defined women's place within Native American culture as one of some power and authority. Men hunted and provided game to be prepared by their women. They believed that women owned that for which they labored. For example, the lodges belonged to women because they not only tanned the buffalo hides but they also designed and toiled over the lodge's construction. Women owned most of the possessions in the tipi--even the clothes that their men wore.

It was the priests' view that the stature of women in Native American society was an obstacle to acculturation. Father Mengarini wrote that the problem:

> was that women were such masters over their men that the latter were not allowed to manage even the smallest household detail or manner of living. At morning and evening the wife served portions of food to both husband and children. This not infrequently aroused the ire of the husband, for if his wife was displeased with him, he was certain to pass the day without eating, or at best to receive a few animal entrails as would befit a dog.

The sisters worked with the Jesuits to teach Native girls their place as homemakers, while boys learned the skills needed to become the economic provider of a family in white society. Four days a week the girls went to school, where they learned religion; the basics of reading, writing and arithmetic; and domestic arts. The sisters' curriculum divided homemaking skills by year according to apparent difficulty. For example, the girls worked in the kitchen the first year and learned how to wash dishes. In the three years that followed, they learned to prepare and cook vegetables and meats. Besides working in the kitchen, they spent one day a week in either the bakery or the cannery. The girls' academic day also included sewing sessions, where they learned to hem and patch cloth, sew on buttons, make buttonholes, and darn socks. Eventually they learned how to make their own uniforms and other clothing. Providing sewing lessons was made easier by a generous gift from Father De Smet. In 1868, the sisters received needed materials from St. Louis. Among the goods was a sewing machine and cloth donated by De Smet to facilitate the sisters' educational labors.

Mary Ronan, the wife of the Indian agent, lauded the work of the sisters in educating Native American girls to perform domestic chores. After the Ronans arrived at the agency in 1877, the sisters sent girls from the boarding school to help the agent's wife with her various household duties. According to Ronan, "From the time of our first going to the agency it was possible to get Indian girls, beautifully trained by the Sisters at St. Ignatius, who helped me with plain sewing and who could be trusted as nursemaids with my children."

While the sisters trained girls in elements of household management, the Jesuit fathers instructed boys in the industries that would enable them to be self-sufficient in white culture. Native American boys, however, learned from their parents the necessary survival skills to maintain their culture, and this hampered missionary efforts. Native American parents educated their sons in the arts of manhood, which emphasized hunting and warfare. Before puberty, boys learned to track game and to set snares. They developed skills in using the bow and arrow. Boys' economic training began in earnest with the voice changes that generally marked puberty. At this time, they were instructed in the care of horses, the killing, skinning, and butchering of bison, and the use and care of weapons.

Parents educated their sons in the responsibilities of manhood while the missionaries attempted to instruct them how to farm and garden. The Catholics' biggest obstacle was in trying to educate Native American boys to embrace industrial occupations in an environment where their families relied on hunting to supplement meager government rations. The Flatheads were not accustomed to agricultural pursuits, men considered cultivation of fields to be women's work. While bison were still plentiful, men continued seasonal hunting, and their sons usually accompanied them. Because of this, boys' attendance at the day school was erratic, and teachers could accomplish little. The girls attended the sisters' boarding school and were separated from their parents and the influence of Native American culture. Not until 1881 did the Jesuits have the financial resources to build a boarding school for boys. In 1883, the fathers built industrial shops where the boys learned the trades of smithy, carpenter, harness maker, cobbler, and printer. The Jesuits also taught seeding and harvesting of crops and the principles of irrigation.

The missionaries added musical training to the curriculum as a recreational outlet and a necessary requirement for religious ceremonies. After their first contact with the Flatheads, the Jesuits observed that music was an important part of Native American life. Most Native groups had a distinctive music that set them apart from one another. The rhythm and voice modulations were designed to "inspire in them an incredible courage when battling their enemies." Music was thought to be an ideal activity for children at the mission. They used it as a replacement for the children's out-of-door life-style and to break the routine of a structured environment. The missionaries perceived that Native American children displayed different musical talents. The sisters trained the girls to sing in the choir at mass and evening prayer. The fathers trained the boys to play in a brass band that accompanied the girls' choir at religious ceremonies.

In the structured boarding school environment, the missionaries closely supervised the children to keep attention on educational training and away from temptations offered outside of the school experience. The missionaries often resorted to corporal punishment to enforce desired behavior. One particular behavior problem occurred in 1872 when the sisters noticed that two girls were making numerous trips to the water well. They investigated and found that the girls were secretly meeting boys. The Jesuit fathers summoned the elders to punish the boys by public whipping. It was customary on the reservation for the missionaries to confer with Native American men, especially the chief, in matters that concerned Native American life. Before white contact, the chief was considered the father of the whole tribe and, therefore, could punish as a father would his children. He disciplined his people for various public crimes such as wife-stealing, murder, theft, and slander. The punishment for these crimes was public whipping. Children were punished by their parents. However, whipping was not administered to children under eight years old for fear that the experience would make them ill-tempered.

When the priests appealed to the Flathead men to administer punishment to the boys for disobeying school rules, the men believed that the girls were as guilty and should receive the same punishment. The girls were taken to the sisters' house where a blanket was placed on the floor for them to lie upon while they each received twenty strokes. The punishment did not stop the girls from sneaking away. Because the children did not always change their behavior after being punished, the sisters concluded that it was not within Native American culture to respond to corrective stimulus as it was in white culture. One of the sisters stated that "the heart of an Indian is not too sensitive to honor of an act. He does not feel it as a white person would."

Assimilation of Native American children into white culture was complete when they were old enough to marry, establish their own homes, and take financial care of their families. Before this was possible, the Jesuits believed that they needed to change aspects of Flathead culture that they perceived to be evil and contributing to what they considered the savage nature of Native American society. Flathead marriage practices were particularly offensive to the priests. The Flatheads recognized three forms of marriage rites, wedding by public acknowledgment of cohabitation, wedding by parental exhortation, and wedding by marriage song and dance. The marriage contract was an agreement between families, not just between the couple. It was the beginning of an extended relationship that included sharing of hunting, camping, and economic resources. In the event that a man or woman died, the extended family provided a new mate. If the wife died, it was common for the husband to marry one of his wife's younger sisters. In the same manner, the brother of a deceased husband married his brother's wife. This marriage relationship often resulted in polygamy where some men, in order to accommodate more than one family, had two or more separate lodges.

The Jesuits, recognizing only one legitimate marriage rite sanctified by the Church, believed that the Flatheads did not understand the commitment of the union of man and woman as prescribed by God. Polygamy was particularly offensive. It bothered them that Native Americans did not always stay with the same marriage partner. According to Father De Smet, "We have not found, even among the best disposed, who, after marriage had been contracted in their own fashion, did not believe himself justified in sending away his first wife, whenever he thought fit, and taking another." The Flatheads were not as casual in discarding their marriage partners as the Jesuits perceived. They believed that there were certain acceptable conditions under which to obtain a divorce. The major causes were adultery, economic failure of the husband, and neglect by the woman of her household. If a woman was physically abused by her husband, her family had the right to take her away. The missionaries instructed Native Americans of the need for Christian marriages and practices. If a man had more than one wife, then the priests instructed him to cast all but one out of his lodge. The one who was to stay was the one with whom he had fathered the most children. It is not clear what happened to the unfortunate woman with fewer children. When the Jesuits were assured of the relationship between each couple, they then performed the marriage ceremony. In this way, the missionaries sought to destroy the traditional Native American family structure of kin relationships. It was also important that Native American families live independently of one another and not share communal lands. The missionaries assumed that by enforcing Christian marriages and educating Native American youth to their "proper" role as husband and wife, the Flathead people would abandon their traditional culture and live prosperously in the white world.

At the boarding schools the missionaries encouraged Native American youths to practice Victorian courtship and marriage rituals. Boys formally visited young girls in the boarding school parlor. When they married, the sisters gave the girls a trousseau, a couple of chickens, and a cow. The boys received a horse. The missionaries expected that the married couple would build their own home, set up housekeeping, and farm according to the training provided by the missionaries. To facilitate acculturation, the Indian agent proposed that the government furnish for each couple their own land, plowed acreage, and house and outbuildings. This gift required that the young couple set up housekeeping away from their parents. By maintaining a separation from Native American parents, missionaries believed that Native American young people would cease practicing their culture and customs. To reinforce boarding school training, the sisters made regular visits to the new homes, where they offered help with household problems.

Although providing academic and religious instruction was part of the sisters' missionary role in acculturation, attending to the medical needs of Native Americans was more in line with the purpose of their foundation. Of the four sisters stationed at the mission, both Sister Mary Edouard and Sister Mary of the Infant Jesus had sufficient medical knowledge to nurse and prescribe medicines. They diagnosed ailments and prescribed remedies that consisted of combinations of plants and roots. Physicians from the School of Medicine at the University of Victoria in Montreal prepared a medical book for the Sisters of Providence in 1869. The book, entitled *Traite Elementaire de Matiere Medicale*, included the Latin and common names of plants and their properties, uses, and dosage. For example, a typical entry such as Dracontium Foetidum, or Skunk Cabbage, listed the qualities of the plant and its use as a stimulant, expectorant, and narcotic. The plant was recommended for asthma, rheumatism, epilepsy, and similar ailments. Other important information included recommended dosage and the method of administration.

Homeopathic medicine, as practiced by the sisters, was similar to the medicine used by the Flatheads. Tribal "physicians" had knowledge of herbal lore and prescribed plants and roots to their patients. Before white contact, they did not suffer serious and devastating diseases. Their ailments were mostly colds, coughs, stomach aches, and illness caused by too much meat or vegetable matter in the diet. They treated these ailments using plants common to their environment. For example, they used chewable roots and peppermint for colds and stomach aches, and made teas from flowers and fir needles for coughs and general weakness. Most Native American remedies were not effective in treating disease after white contact. Some anthropologists believe that the smallpox epidemic of 1781-1782 and "fever and ague" of 1830-1831 reduced Native American population of the Northwest by 80 percent. Added to these epidemics was the introduction of tuberculosis, measles, and sexually transmitted diseases.

The "magic" of medicine men and shamans had very little effect on these diseases. One way in which the missionaries won the Flatheads' confidence was by demonstrating that the power of the missionaries' medicine was stronger than that of the Native people. To eliminate the influence of medicine men, the Jesuits needed to convince the Flatheads that the missionary's medicine would help them live a long life. Father Anthony Ravalli, who studied medicine in Turin, Italy, worked among the different tribes in the Northwest from 1845 until his death at St. Mary's Mission in 1884. Ravalli brought with him a vaccine for smallpox that helped save Native American lives. He experimented with the herbs used by Native Americans and concluded that they were of little value. He relied on his own knowledge to secure medicines and learned how to make alcohol from camas root. In this way, the missionaries replaced the function of the medicine man and facilitated culture change to accommodate Christian doctrine. On the reservation, the Flatheads came to rely on the missionaries. The sisters administered their herbal remedies to the sick in their convent and also traveled throughout the reservation, sometimes covering distances over thirty-five miles to care for Native Americans in their homes.

Providing a hospital for Native Americans was part of the 1855 Stevens treaty. Just as federal funds were not made available for schools, there was no appropriation for the building and maintenance of a hospital on the reservation. The Sisters of Providence sought the opportunity to establish a hospital in Missoula, a mining town and military post forty-five miles south of the mission. The opportune time came in 1873 while Mother Caron was visiting St. Ignatius. Evidently the mother superior's visit was extended throughout the winter because of a mishap in which she fell and broke her arm. While convalescing during the long winter, she witnessed the isolation and apparent loneliness of the sisters.

Mother Caron was the first from the Sisters of Providence in Vancouver or Montreal to visit the sisters at St. Ignatius in seven years. The sisters' loneliness was made greater by the length of time it took to receive any communication from their families. It sometimes took over a year for mail to arrive from Montreal, and even longer from Vancouver, even though Vancouver was closer to the mission than the eastern Canadian city. It was Mother Caron's belief that by establishing another branch of their foundation in Missoula, they would incorporate more sisters from their congregation to administer to the sick and needy. That, in turn, would provide opportunities for the sisters at St. Ignatius to have a change of environment and contact with a non-Indian community. The additional sisters would help also to reinforce religious obligations and discipline. One of the things that concerned Mother Caron during her visit was that the sisters were no longer wearing the traditional habit. Instead, they were wearing moccasins and denim dresses.

In keeping with the practice of consulting the authority of the Church hierarchy, Mother Caron sought permission to establish a new foundation from her councilors in Montreal and Father Giorda. The councilors readily approved her plan, but Father Giorda was hesitant to give his consent. The Jesuit maintained that he did not have any priests available for the Missoula mission and, therefore, the sisters would not have anyone to minister the sacraments to them. The Jesuits did, however, issue funds to secure land and a house for the sisters that would be available to them when Father Giorda believed the time was right for an expansion of Catholic institutions. Mother Caron, undaunted by Jesuit objections, arranged to have her sisters moved to the newly purchased mission house before she returned to Montreal. The sisters accepted the sacrifice of only having a priest visit them once a month.

The house that the Jesuits bought for the sisters' new foundation in Missoula had previously served as a courthouse, a school house, and lastly, a chicken roost. It was in such poor condition that snow drifted in during the winter months. Another obstacle to the sisters' comfort was the lack of water. For this necessity, the sisters had to walk almost a half mile to the near by river. Seeing the sisters' situation, members of the mining community dug a canal from the sisters' house to the river. However, domestic animals contaminated the water. Eventually, the sisters established a routine in which they arose before dawn to haul water to their convent cellar, where in summer months they could keep it cool for the day. Besides water, the sisters' diet consisted of bread, salt pork, and tea. The Jesuit lay brothers helped the sisters by making straw tick beds, a table, and four chairs. Empty crates made up the rest of the furniture.

The greatest obstacle the sisters encountered in Missoula was lack of money. Even though government appropriations were not always reliable, government money helped to maintain the convent at St. Ignatius. The Missoula foundation was not an Indian mission; therefore, government funds were not available for operation and maintenance of the hospital. To support their convents at both locations, the sisters continued collection tours to mining districts and divided the money between the two foundations. The money enabled them to visit the sick in their homes and to care for patients in their small convent hospital, which accommodated twelve patients in the first year. The sisters also received a contract for the care of the county poor. In 1874, they collected enough money from the mines to establish St. Patrick's Hospital. They eventually supported the hospital and other charitable works with the revenue from patients.

The Sisters of Providence went to St. Ignatius in 1864 with the expectation that they would care for and educate Native American children who lived in ignorance of a civilized world and a Christian God. The Jesuits expected that the sisters would not only educate Native American children but also provide, by their very presence, an industrious example of women's sphere to Native American girls. The success of their programs to educate and convert the Flathead children was only possible as long as the two religious orders could maintain a building program and secure financial resources for daily operations. Ultimately, to meet these pecuniary demands, the Catholic missionaries relied on the federal government to support their programs in Native American acculturation.

3

THE TRAIL TO
THE GREAT WHITE FATHER

The Jesuits and Sisters of Providence built St. Ignatius Mission into a model institution for the education of Native American children. Senator George G. Vest of Missouri, a member of the United States Senate's special committee to investigate Indian mission schools, praised Catholic missionary programs to educate and convert the Flathead children. Vest, after visiting St. Ignatius in 1884, considered that the Catholics achieved unprecedented success in transforming Native American boys into farmers and Native American girls into Victorian homemakers. He spoke of the merits of Catholic education before the Senate in his appeal for a continuance of congressional appropriations for Indian mission schools. Vest believed that those students who achieved the highest degree of cultural integration were those who had very little contact with their families and lived at the mission boarding schools. It was the Senator's opinion that money given to government day schools was wasted money. The only schools worth maintaining were boarding schools such as those the Catholics established at their Indian missions. Catholic missionaries fought continually for federal appropriations to establish and maintain their schools. Friends of their cause like Senator Vest facilitated their efforts to gain financial support from the federal government. Foes, however, greatly outnumbered friends.

Government funds to support the sisters' boarding school were inconsistent and unreliable. The uncertainty arose from the Indian policy recommended by President Ulysses S. Grant. Under pressure from humanitarian groups known as "friends of the Indians," Grant called for a more humane Indian policy than had existed in the early nineteenth century. The President's peace policy authorized Congress to establish the Board of Indian Commissioners. The board, made up of Protestant laymen, functioned as an advisory committee to the Bureau of Indian Affairs and supervised the appropriation of funds to Indian agencies. Another aspect of Grant's policy was to allow missionary societies to appoint different religious denominations to take charge of reservation agencies and, in turn, to appoint the Indian agent. There were a total of seventy-two agencies among the different Indian tribes. The Catholics were the first to establish missions at thirty-eight of these agencies, and they expected to maintain them and to continue serving over 100,000 Native American Catholics. But, even though it was President Grant's proposal that agencies be assigned to missionary groups already working among the tribes, the Catholics received only eight agencies. Protestant denominations, who claimed only 15,000 Native American Christians, received the majority. The result of this allocation was that 80,000 Native American Catholics could no longer receive Church sacraments. In response to Protestant management of federal Indian policy, Catholic bishops established the Bureau of Catholic Indian Missions (BCIM) in 1874. The BCIM became a lobbying force in Washington. The Bureau's objectives were to direct the administration of Catholic agencies, to reestablish authority at Catholic agencies then under Protestant control, to continue ministering to Native American Catholics, and to procure financial resources to establish schools and provide teachers.

Government appropriation of funds to Indian missions also favored Protestant denominations. For example, Congress allocated funds according to a contract between the government and the mission school, which stated the per capita allowance for the agreed number of students enrolled. The amount issued by the government to Catholic missionaries was low in comparison to funding allocated for government and non-Catholic denominational schools. These schools received federal funds for buildings, furnishings, and equipment as well as the salaries of administrators, teachers, and other employees. Along with this funding, they received a per capita allowance for each student. Catholic schools only received a per capita amount for each student. This inequitable system concerned the missionaries at St. Ignatius because they believed that under the new system, the funding allocated for schools on the reservation would be diverted to denominations that chose to establish a mission on the Flathead Reservation. Their fear was that the Methodists would build a church and school at Taho Agency, and federal money would be diverted to the Protestants. As one Jesuit remarked, "get the little salary for school which salary now goes to the sisters, who have nothing else to clothe board and teach some twenty Native American girls, who are improving a great deal under their motherly care." The sporadic and low allocation of funding for St. Ignatius caused the missionaries to lobby aggressively to the mission board in charge in Indian agencies for Indian agents who were sympathetic to their efforts to acculturate Native Americans.

The Indian agent was an important link between the government and mission schools because he was responsible for the allocation of government money and he supervised government employees. The government hired the priests, nuns, and other workers at the mission to carry out the 1855 treaty agreements—operation of a school and agricultural pursuits. Technically, then, the missionaries were government employees under the authority of the Indian agent. So, it was in the missionaries' interest to work with Indian agents sympathetic to the Catholic cause. Between 1872 and 1877, the missionaries considered the agents assigned to St. Ignatius Mission unscrupulous characters who did little about instituting educational programs that would transform Native Americans into Christian farm families. The missionaries found it difficult to assert their independence at the mission when they were under the thumb of the Indian agent. And the agents believed that they were the reservation authority, and that included jurisdiction over the mission and missionaries. As can be imagined, the arrangement caused conflict between missionaries and agents resulting in a power struggle in which the Catholics fought for the continuance and livelihood of the mission establishment. There was irony in this struggle. The Flathead Reservation was one of the agencies assigned to the Catholics under Grant's peace policy. The Bureau of Indian Affairs, therefore, sent Catholic agents to supervise the reservation.

The missionaries' main concern was that the agent would distribute promised annuities to the mission school and would work to increase the number of boarding schools and pupils in attendance. The missionaries could easily discern between the qualities of a "good" Catholic agent, who recognized the benefit of Catholic education for Native Americans, and a Catholic who "fell by the wayside" and saw to his own self-interest. Father Giorda made such a judgment in a testimonial letter for Flathead agent, Major C.S. Jones, who left the employment of the agency in 1872. Father Giorda stated that Jones "endeared himself to all our missionaries and to his Indian charges so well. His upright character, his sobriety and honesty made us to love in him a true Christian gentleman." The missionaries worked so well with Jones that Father Van Gorp wrote the BCIM that they should recommend Jones for appointment to "the office of Supervisor of Indian Affairs." Van Gorp pointed out that President Grant had promised the position to a Catholic. They considered Jones the perfect candidate because "he has worked hand in hand with the missionaries to ameliorate the spiritual and material condition of the Indians." The missionaries were very disappointed when the Bureau of Indian Affairs appointed Major D. Shanahan as Jones's successor at the agency. Even though Shanahan was a Catholic, the missionaries developed an acrimonious relationship with him. The bone of contention between the two parties was the placement of the school for Native American children. In the Jesuits' opinion, the agent conspired to establish an educational facility at the agency and not at the mission, thereby undermining the authority of the missionaries. The missionaries believed that in doing this the agent schemed to disestablish the mission and diminish its influence. The missionaries applied pressure to the government, through the BCIM, for complete control of schools on the reservation. One way to establish this control was to engage in an ambitious building program that would hopefully secure Catholic domination over Native American education and acculturation.

The sisters and Jesuits proposed to the BCIM that provisions be made for the building of another boarding school at the mission to house forty boys, and that the number of girls and per capita allowance be increased at the sisters' boarding school. The sisters wanted the Bureau to pressure the federal government for the establishment of a hospital as stipulated in the Stevens treaty. The most immediate concern, however, was for the Bureau to investigate the irregular payment of teachers' salaries. As employees of the federal government, the sisters received a salary, which they used for the support of the girls attending the boarding school. The sisters believed that they did not receive the funds because the superintendent in Washington was prejudiced against Catholics. Regardless of whether there was such a prejudice among the employees of the Bureau of Indian Affairs, the Catholics at St. Ignatius believed that agent Shanahan needed to be removed because he was not distributing annuities to Native Americans or allocating funds to the missionaries. Under Grant's policy, the missionaries believed that they could call for the removal of an inefficient agent, and they urged the BCIM to look into the matter. The missionaries eventually drafted charges against Shanahan which, with affidavits from witnesses, claimed that the agent took $400 worth of blankets issued to Native Americans and sold them to a storekeeper, who in turn charged the Indians $7.00 a pair. They also accused him of gambling, drinking, and displaying immoral conduct. After Shanahan disappeared from the reservation for a couple of months, the missionaries were convinced that he was going to be replaced. But, after several months absence, he returned and confronted the fathers, challenging their accusations against him. He then began removing government employees and claiming budget problems. He fired the wagon maker and the assistant miller. He suspended Father Bandini, who taught at the boys' day school, and Sister Remi and Sister Paul Miki from the girls' school. Shanahan's motivation for suspending the missionaries is not altogether clear. His report to the Commissioners of Indian Affairs stated that he was allocating money for improvements at the agency, and that he had "retained only those hands for the purpose of building Agency improvements" because no "extra funds" had been "placed to my credit with which to pay them." Shanahan's concern for improvements at the Agency was consistent with the wishes of the people on the Flathead Reservation.

The struggle over whether the federal government appropriated money for a school at the agency or at the mission seventeen miles away overshadowed the interests of the Flatheads. While the missionaries struggled to maintain the mission schools, the Flatheads urged the federal government to establish the school at the agency as stipulated in the Stevens treaty. The Flatheads also questioned why the missionaries only had a school for girls; the chiefs insisted that they wanted a school for boys. Agent Shanahan argued the chiefs' case in his written defense of suspending the missionaries. He related to officials the results of a council held by the chiefs of the Confederated Tribes, where the chiefs "urgently requested the agent to open a school at this agency, in accordance with the treaty saying that after so many years not one of their boys could be found who could intelligently read or write the English language."

The Flatheads who lived fifty miles south in the Bitterroot Valley refused to move north to the reservation in the Flathead Valley because of broken treaty agreements, especially the promise of schools. In 1872, Congressman James A. Garfield negotiated another treaty to remove the Flatheads from the Bitterroot. Again, the federal government made promises that were not kept. Among the long list of complaints registered by the chiefs was the violation of the fifth article of the Stevens treaty promising the establishment and maintenance of a school. Arlee, chief of the Flatheads, testified that when he met with Garfield he

> did not want to move down to the Jocko Reservation [Flathead Reservation] but Garfield promised us that we should have a public school according to the old treaty, I was glad when he promised this. But we have no school. There is a school at a mission, seventeen miles away, but it is no benefit to the tribe. They educate girls there but not boys ... we want our boys educated not our girl ... we want a school at the agency according to the treaty ... we have asked this of the Agent, but he has only told us that our school is at the mission.

Indian sentiment was again expressed when Chief Arlee and Chief Michelle of the Pend d'Oreilles appeared before the United States Grand Jury in 1876. The chiefs registered a complaint against their new agent, Charles Medary, for mismanagement of the agency and against the federal government for failure to fulfill treaty obligations. Subsequently, Medary was removed as agent and replaced by Major Peter Ronan in 1877. The relationship between the missionaries and Ronan, a devout Catholic, was congenial and productive. The Indians, however, had to accept the mission school for the education of their girls and wait for several years for a similar facility for the boys. A year after Ronan became agent, the government raised the contract allowance for the mission school to $4,000, and it stayed at that level until 1890.

Through the efforts of agent Ronan, the BCIM, and charitable donations, the Catholics at St. Ignatius were able to implement a vigorous building program. In 1881, the missionaries built two school boarding houses, one for the boys and one for the girls. The sisters' school was 45x50 feet with a French roof. The sisters were able to maintain their new school with the new regular quarterly allowance secured by agent Ronan for the mission school. The missionaries expanded the boarding schools in 1883 with the expectation that the government would increase the number of students and per capita allowance as well. Father Van Gorp wrote Father Brouillet at the BCIM explaining such a plan, and Father Brouillet and the Commissioner of Indian Affairs agreed on a new contract that increased the number of girls at the sisters' boarding school to fifty. The contract with the fathers allowed for enrollment of thirty boys.

In addition, to the enrollment of children from the Flathead, Pend d' Oreille, and Kutenai tribes, in 1884 the Jesuits accepted the request of Father Prando, who worked with the Blackfeet in central Montana, that the missionaries at St. Ignatius make room at the boarding schools for fifty Blackfoot children, who were terribly undernourished and evidently near starvation. The winter of 1884 was a desperate time for many Native Americans who lived on the Plains of Eastern Montana. The harsh winter took its toll on livestock that was the main food source for most people. Understanding the urgency of the situation, Father Prando immediately sought the approval of the Blackfoot agent for the removal of the Blackfoot children. Once the missionaries received permission to transfer the students, the Commissioner of Indian Affairs helped the missionaries by approving extra appropriations to accommodate the new students. The unfortunate conditions that led to the difficult survival of the Blackfoot in 1884 fortuitously provided an opportunity for the missionaries at St. Ignatius to expand their programs to more Native American children. After Father Prando escorted the first group of children to St. Ignatius in August, he observed, "The process of civilizing for those Indians will be materially helped by being in contact with other Indians already to a great extent civilized."

In 1890, the Catholics devised a trial education program that would supplement the boarding school experience. The Jesuits instituted a kindergarten at the mission to board Native American children as young as two years old. By removing children this young from their families, the missionaries believed that they would be more successful in eliminating the influence of Native American culture. The Indian agent also encouraged the idea of a kindergarten. In trying to obtain added government appropriations for the establishment of a kindergarten boarding school, Peter Ronan wrote the Commissioner of Indian Affairs that

> the children if taken into school at the age of two or three years and kept there, only occasionally visited by the parents, will, when grown up, know nothing of Indian ways and habits. They will with ease, and thoroughly, become perceptibly formed to the ways of the whites in their habits, their thoughts, their aspirations, etc. They will not know in fact be completely ignorant of the Indian language. Will know only English. One generation will accomplish what now it takes many generations to effect. The affection of the child being gained at its young age, it is likely to grow up with love for the whites instead of the hatred or at least diffidence, as is the case to a great extent at present.

By Catholic accounts, the mothers were willing and even enthusiastic about turning over their young children to the missionaries. It is difficult to imagine that parents who gave up their children to the missionaries, no matter what their motives, did not display the apparent antagonism held by the parents towards the whites mentioned in Peter Ronan's report to the Commissioner. The parents were seldom allowed to visit their children; and when they did, they could not communicate with them because the children spoke only English. The parents were forced to converse with their children through an interpreter.

The establishment of a mission kindergarten renewed animosity between the Sisters of Providence and the Jesuits because the priests asked the Ursuline Nuns, who had established Indian mission schools on reservations in central and eastern Montana, to run the new school at St. Ignatius instead of the Sisters of Providence. The reason, perhaps, for this bold move on the part of the Jesuits was that the Ursulines were more accommodating to the division of work at the mission than the Sisters of Providence. For example, Father Cataldo wrote an agreement with the Ursulines that outlined their duties at the mission and the responsibilities of the Jesuits. The contract stipulated that the Ursulines would provide the "necessary care and services for the successful carrying on of a kindergarten." It was also agreed that the sisters would "see to the washing and mending of the clothes of the Fathers community and of the boys of the boarding school." In return for these services, the fathers agreed to "furnish the necessary buildings for the sisters and those under their charge, the same being and remaining the property of the fathers" and that the fathers agreed to "supply and provide all that is required for the running of said institution, i.e. boarding, clothing, etc. of the sisters and the children and to pay for whatever outside help may be deemed necessary."

The contract agreement with the Ursulines clearly suggests that the Jesuits believed that women religious should take care of the fathers' domestic chores. The Sisters of Providence had worked hard to free themselves of this responsibility. In so doing, there arose a general feeling of antagonism between the two orders. The Ursulines, however, accepted the paternalistic care of the fathers and, in turn, agreed to the fathers' personal care. There is no evidence that there was animosity between the Sisters of Providence and the Ursulines in their respective efforts to educate Native American children. The Sisters of Providence did, however, believe that the Jesuits were trying to destroy their school when they helped the Ursulines start a kindergarten at the mission. The Sisters of Providence were upset when the Jesuits withdrew $42 from the per capita allowance allocated to them and gave it to the Ursulines for the maintenance of the new community. Younger girls from the Sisters of Providence's school attended the new kindergarten, which reduced further the sisters' government appropriation. Complicating the financial hardship was the fathers' insistence that the older girls from the sisters' school assist in the Ursuline laundry. The Sisters of Providence accused the fathers of enticing the girls away with financial rewards. The sisters needed the older girls to help them with the younger girls at their school.

Regardless of the sometimes antagonistic relationship between the Sisters of Providence and the Jesuits, the three religious orders were successful in promoting religious and educational excellence at St. Ignatius in the 1890s. They built the mission into a model agency of Native American acculturation. The missionaries accomplished this by taking advantage of the government contract system for mission schools. It was always in the interest of the Catholics to initiate building programs that would increase the size of boarding schools and, therefore, the number of students. The BCIM, then, lobbied for increased enrollment of students at mission schools and an increase in allowance per student. In 1890, the per capita allowance was raised from $8.50 to $12.50. The Catholics were so successful at increasing enrollment at their schools that the Protestants, alarmed at the growing Catholic influence on reservations, applied pressure to Congress to discontinue government subsidies to sectarian schools even if it meant cutting funds to Protestant missions. The increase in foreign immigration in the 1880s and 1890s from eastern European and predominately Catholic countries caused an outbreak of nativism and anti-Catholicism. The Protestants equated Catholic education on reservations with immigrants who reinforced their cultural identity by practicing old country customs and who insisted on speaking their native language. To the Protestants, the Americanization of Native Americans should be modeled after American principles inherent to New England Protestantism.

The government could not drastically cut appropriations to Indian missions without interrupting Indian education. The plan was to provide a transition period during which students would be slowly integrated into government industrial schools. From 1896 to 1900, Congress debated the issue of appropriations for mission schools. Protestants used the argument that government funding of religious schools on reservations violated the doctrine of separation of church and state. The BCIM lobbied unsuccessfully during these years for the continuance of the contract system. In 1900, Congress passed the last appropriation bill for funding religious schools on reservations. Without government funding, the missionaries at St. Ignatius had a difficult time maintaining the complex of schools with an enrollment of over 320 students. In 1901, the BCIM allocated $8,640 for the support of 80 students. After this date, however, the Bureau was unable to fund education at the mission. To raise funds for the mission, Father Cataldo traveled throughout the East lecturing and delivering sermons on behalf of the schools. He was only able to collect $3,000 to be divided among the schools. The lack of funds caused the Jesuits to reduce the number of students and to cut educational programs. Adding to the difficulties of fiscal maintenance was an unfortunate series of fires that further handicapped the missionaries. In 1896, a fire destroyed the boys' school and dormitory. The missionaries believed that one of the boys deliberately set fire to a mattress. In 1919, fire destroyed all the buildings of the Sisters of Providence. The order decided not to rebuild, thus ending fifty-five years of educational work at the mission. The sisters, however, stayed at the mission administering Holy Family Hospital, established in 1914. Their work at Holy Family was more in line with the original dictate of their order, to provide care for the sick and needy. In 1922, fire destroyed the Ursulines' school and convent. The Ursulines rebuilt their school and took over the work started by the Sisters of Providence in educating Native American children at St. Ignatius. By so doing, the Ursulines continued their heritage of educating both Indian and white girls, which began in 1884 when the Jesuits invited the sisters to establish schools among the Plains Indians.

Sister Ignatius McFarland, Mother Amadeus Dunne, Sister Sacred Heart Meilink, Sister Mary Angela Abair, Sister Frances Seifert, Sister Holy Angels Carabin. Sitting for photo before leaving Toledo convent for Miles City, 1884. Courtesy of Ursuline Convent, Toledo, Ohio.

4

THE TRAIL TO MILES CITY

The temperature was below zero when Mother Amadeus and five Ursuline Nuns arrived in Miles City in 1884. The sisters were the first from the Ursuline order who volunteered to leave the comfort and sanctity of their convent home in Ohio to establish mission schools on the Cheyenne, Crow, Blackfoot, and Gros Ventre-Assiniboine Reservations in central and eastern Montana. The Ursulines, like many women missionaries who went west in the nineteenth century, dedicated their lives to bringing their religion and their civilization to Native Americans. In so doing, the sisters' assumptions about their roles as women religious changed over time to accommodate their experiences in a new environment and their role as missionaries.

The invitation extended to the Ursulines to establish schools among the Plains Indians came from an appeal by Fathers Prando and Barcelo, who were proselytizing among the Crows and Cheyennes. It was their contention that if the Catholics did not hurry and establish missions with these tribes, the Protestants would. In a letter to the Jesuit superior of the Rocky Mountain Missions, Father Prando advised,

> The Protestant minister who lives three miles from Miles City is preparing to establish himself among the Cheyennes. Father Lindesmith and the interpreter believe it necessary that we leave as soon as possible to preclude

the progress of such a minister. We concluded that when the mission be given to the priest and five sisters we shall leave.

Prando considered the situation urgent and believed that sisters somehow legitimized the Catholic claim to establish their institutions among the Cheyennes.

Bishop Brondel contacted Bishop Gilmore in Cleveland, Ohio requesting that he ask nuns in his diocese to volunteer as missionaries to the Cheyenne people. Gilmore placed an advertisement in the diocesan newspaper, *The Universe*, soliciting volunteers. Thirty Ursuline Nuns from Toledo petitioned for missionary duty. Out of the thirty, Gilmore chose six whom he thought could withstand the hardships of missionary life on the frontier. Bishop Gilmore instructed the sisters that their responsibility was to establish two communities of their order, one among the residents in Miles City and the other among the Cheyennes. On January 15, 1884, Mother Amadeus, along with Sisters Sacred Heart, Ignatius, Holy Angels, St. Angela, and St. Francis, left Toledo for Miles City. Accompanying them was Father E.H. Eyler, who planned to assume ministerial duties at the new mission. Bishop Gilmore appointed Mother Amadeus as superior of the Montana Ursulines.

When the sisters left Toledo, they were not aware of the hardships and experiences that they would encounter in working to establish and maintain Indian mission schools. Their trip by train from Toledo to Miles City illustrates their naivete concerning what was in store for them as western pioneers. Their departure was a "gala day" because of the excitement in finally securing the necessary money and passes for their trip. Once on the train, the sisters sought to maintain a certain decorum suitable to their profession. They purposely occupied the drawing room of the sleeper car, which provided them with seclusion and "no eyes to cast curious but respectful glances." They were also anxious for privacy so that they could enjoy the contents of the hamper that Mother Stanislaus, Toledo Superior, had packed for them. What Mother Stanislaus provided for her girls was a large hamper and six baskets full of food and assorted items that she believed to be necessities. It was a gesture of warmth and affection from a mother whose children were leaving home for the first time. Sister Sacred Heart confessed the sisters took "such consolation from our never failing friend, The Hamper. Oh, how we enjoyed the biscuit and butter, the cheese, (I could not cut it fast enough), the chicken and jelly, the chipped beef and that 'that cheers the heart.'" Besides the feast sent from Toledo, the sisters' meals in the dining car suited their insatiable appetites. They ate in the

> Palace Dining Car, no misnomer ... Delmonico himself could not have furnished a more luxurious meal. The waiters, in their white coats and aprons, showed their ivorys [sic], as though a little surprised at their quests, but soon discovered that we were able to keep them pretty busy. Oh Mother we enjoyed our breakfast as well as every visit to the dining car so much ... We were more rested when the journey had ended than when we entered the car in Toledo.

The change in landscape was a sobering experience that perhaps awakened the sisters to the realities of their decision to become missionaries. Sister Sacred Heart commented,

> In my mind the country seemed so barren and deserted. For miles not a single house or sign of any living creature, then perhaps a few scattered houses bearing the name of a town. The rest one vast wilderness, covered with snow at this time of season, not a single tree anywhere, sometimes a few shrubs struggling for existence in the bed of a little stream.

While the sisters were following the change of scenery as the train advanced westward, they were also on the lookout for Indians. They had never seen Native American people and were curious about what they looked like. They kept a watchful eye, often speculating about who would see one first. Once settled at their boarding house in Miles City, Sister Sacred Heart wrote, "I went to the door, saw someone copper colored splitting wood in the yard before me and without waiting to have a second glance rushed into the room exclaiming, Oh I saw the Indian first. Imagine the laugh that followed when the nuns came to the door and saw John Chinaman with his long cue gracefully twisted on the back of his head."

Bishop Brondel and Reverend Eligh Lindesmith, Army Chaplain at Fort Keogh, met the sisters at the station when they arrived in Miles City three days after leaving Toledo. The town, founded in 1877 as a supply depot for nearby Fort Keogh, was rough, with few amenities. In 1883, the citizens formed a vigilante group to clean up the town. After an individual of questionable character insulted a woman on the street, the group hanged the fellow. That night friends of the victim burned down a good portion of Miles City. The following day, the vigilantes unburdened the town of all undesirable characters. When the sisters arrived a year later, the town had a few substantial homes, a couple of merchandise stores, and a reported sixty-five saloons.

The sisters' new home in Montana was a great departure from the security of their cloistered convent in Ohio. The six nuns were on their own and the bishop and Jesuits expected them to be economically and physically self-sufficient. This became apparent their first night in Miles City. Before the sisters left Toledo, Father Lindesmith assured Bishop Gilmore in Cleveland that the sisters would have a suitable place to rent or buy in Miles City. However, there were no accommodations waiting for the sisters and the best the fathers could do was to recommend a room at Bridget McCanna's boarding house. Mother Amadeus described the residence as a "white-washed log cabin with a Chinese laundry attached-- Yelee Laundry." Their first, and last, night at the boarding house was very cold because their room did not have a stove. To make conditions worse, snow drifted in through the ill-fitting doors and windows. One sister believed that Mrs. McCanna had recently used the room for a chicken coop. "Not only the smell made us think so but the straw and feathers that were scattered here and there." Father Eyler was indignant about the sisters' lodgings. "He could not stay ten minutes in the room for the dirt of the place annoyed him so much ... the odor of the room was to him intolerable." The sisters only had a stretched calico partition between themselves and other boarders whom they described as "ditch diggers, cowboys, and ranchmen." They spent their first night sitting on the floor with their backs against the wall because the beds were a worse alternative.

The next day, the Ursulines searched for a more suitable residence that also would serve as a convent. Out of the customary respect for

Church hierarchy, Mother Amadeus asked Bishop Brondel's permission to find their own lodging. She insisted to Brondel "we could suit ourselves sooner and better than anyone else." The sisters employed a real estate agent who helped them to find a small, five-room house for twenty-five dollars a month. That same day the sisters went shopping for necessities such as stoves for heating and cooking and a supply of coal.

The day of shopping made the sisters aware of the uncultured nature of the frontier town. Sister Sacred Heart commented that "Everyone walks in the middle of the road; it is a better plan, for many people use the side of the street for the slop sink." She also observed that "Every second store is a saloon. We have not met six Catholic men (Montana Catholics they call themselves) who are not saloon keepers, gamblers and the like." Her analysis was that "Christianity is at its lowest ebb here."

The sisters worked straight through their second day and night cleaning and arranging their convent. They set up their stoves and delivered their own coal so they would not have to spend another cold night. In their convent the sisters built a small chapel at the end of one of the rooms. They used the linen napkins and tablecloth from their hampers as altar cloths.

Bishop Brondel stayed four days in Miles City. After the sisters established themselves in their new home, the bishop left for Helena. Before he left, he bestowed on them an unexpected honor. He entrusted them with the care of the Blessed Sacrament. Mother Amadeus explained to Mother Stanislaus,

> Oh, Mother the news is so good that we can hardly wait to tell you. The Bishop gave us permission to have the Blessed Sacrament with us night and day. He came Monday morning with Father Lindesmith and looked all around but you could see by the twinkle in his eye that he was going to do something good for us. He came again in the afternoon and stayed a long time and before he left he said that since we had left our beautiful home and all for God, God must do something for us--that He must give us Himself, and then gave permission for us to have the Blessed Sacrament.

The sisters were certainly a logical choice to watch over and protect the Blessed Sacrament. There was no resident priest appointed to the Miles City Church. Father Lindesmith built the Church on ground given to him by an unidentified citizen. In 1881, he forwarded the ownership to the diocese, then under Omaha jurisdiction. Until the Catholics found a permanent clergyman for the Miles City Church, Lindesmith expanded his duties at Fort Keogh to include occasional ministering of the sacraments to Miles City parishioners. Brondel expected the sisters to protect the Blessed Sacrament until the bishop appointed a permanent priest. For the sisters, it was as if Christ were living with them. They believed that His presence in their tabernacle protected them and provided for their every need. Writing to Mother Stanislaus, Sister St. Francis observed, "Dear Mother, you are already aware of our beautiful chapel, therefore, I will say do not buy us anything, we have all the happiness we can desire in Montana, that is we have the Blessed Sacrament ... I feel confident that God will take care of us for He has been so very, very good." This faith carried them through some difficult times as they moved forward with their plans to establish schools in Miles City and on the reservations.

The Ursulines, however, experienced the same lack of financial resources as the Sisters of Providence at St. Ignatius Mission. The Ursulines' convent and school in Miles City would only be successful if they could generate some income. Ultimately, the sisters planned to support their Miles City community with the tuition from student boarders. But, until there was sufficient enrollment to support a school, the sisters relied on their own skills to acquire financial support. They asked Mother Stanislaus to send them a piano so that Sister Sacred Heart could give music lessons. The way they figured it, there were thirty-seven children on the Sunday school list, and most of those students would take music lessons. There was an urgency to their plea to Mother Stanislaus. Evidently, there was competition in Miles City to capture the music market. Mother Amadeus wrote, "A German Professor of Music from Chicago arrived here just a week before us. His coming is bad for us." Besides music lessons, teaching a foreign language was also a lucrative endeavor. The sisters' academic training at the Ursuline Academy in Toledo included French and German. Mother Amadeus believed that the sisters could make money by providing instruction in these languages. It was her impression that the public school teachers in Miles City wanted to learn the French language.

The Ursulines were not only educated in foreign languages, but in other academic disciplines as well. Their academic training at the Ursuline convent school in Toledo included two levels of instruction--a six year college preparatory course and a four year collegiate degree program. In 1873, the State of Ohio granted the Ursuline convent a charter to offer degrees for college- level work. In the collegiate program, the sisters studied Christian doctrine, rhetoric, philosophy, history of European civilizations, natural science, mathematics, French and German, and penmanship. The school also provided very limited instruction in domestic arts. In their four years of study, their classes in domestic economy consisted of culinary art. The sisters' lack of domestic skills hampered their ability to use these skills to earn financial support. Mother Amadeus recognized that there was a demand for education in domestic arts. But, she could only lament that, "I wish we had someone to teach embroidery."

In March, 1884, the Ursulines enrolled three young girls in the limited space of their convent school. The sisters provided the girls with lessons in beginning math and music. Along with their boarding students, the sisters also instructed a day school. But the heat of summer months limited their teaching schedule and their profits. In August they could teach only during the cool of the morning from eight until eleven. Mother Amadeus recognized that the sisters could not establish a permanent boarding school without the tuition from students. But the question was how to acquire the necessary funds to build a school with so few paying students? As Mother Amadeus stated, the sisters were "deprived of the principal means of helping themselves." Bishop Brondel was generous with what little money he could spare. Before he returned to Helena, he purchased a piece of ground and gave it to the sisters for a building site. Along with this purchase, the bishop gave the sisters $250 for their building fund.

By the end of the summer, there was mounting pressure for Mother Amadeus to find the resources to build a boarding school. The Protestants were erecting a schoolhouse, which cost "$20,000," and was "a two story brick, 40x60." The bishop was, therefore, anxious for the sisters to build, and he donated another $100 toward that goal. Mother Amadeus talked to builders about the cost of materials and discovered that in Miles City pine was the same price as mahogany in the East. Prices were high because of high freight costs. The bishop's recommendation was that the sisters borrow the money. Mother Amadeus wrote a series of letters to Mother Stanislaus in Toledo asking for financial support and recommendations on who might help them procure a loan. She stated that she would like to borrow $5,000 for five years at perhaps 5 to 6 percent interest. She told Mother Stanislaus that if the Mother Superior could not get them a loan, then the Montana Ursulines would ask Sister Sacred Heart's father for the money. As hard as the Montana Superior tried, there was very little help from the Ursulines in Toledo. Mother Stanislaus eventually replied by sending fifty dollars for which the Montana Ursulines were very grateful.

Added to the difficulties of finding the financial resources to build their convent and school was upholding the dictates of their order. The Ursulines practiced the rule of enclosure, which meant that they did not interact with mainstream society. Mother Amadeus enforced the rule of enclosure at the Toledo convent after the Ursuline congregation elected her Mother Superior in 1874. As Mother Superior, she directed her sisters to take up the cloistered way of life, which she patterned after the French Ursulines in Montreal. The rule of enclosure reinforced Mother Amadeus' belief in a traditional life for her nuns where the sisters did not leave their convent without special permission and remained behind grilles when visiting with non-religious. The traditional concept of enclosure was to provide a religious environment where nuns could uphold their vows of poverty, chastity, obedience, and a fourth vow added by the Ursulines, employment in the instruction of young girls. Bishop Brondel expected the sisters to continue to practice their contemplative, enclosed religious life on the frontier. Before he returned to the diocese in Helena, he instructed the sisters to "go everywhere for a few weeks and after that to keep enclosure as strictly as possible." Mother Amadeus' zeal for missionary work, however, transcended the practices of traditional sisterhood. As missionaries in the American West, the sisters found it difficult to maintain a disciplined and routine lifestyle that revolved around prayer and contemplation. For the sisters to accomplish their missionary goals, they had to alter their religious culture so that they could participate in the world outside convent walls.

The Ursulines' financial problems in getting established in Miles City prompted Bishop Brondel to offer them a place with the Jesuit fathers at St. Peter's Mission, which initially served the Blackfoot, Gros Ventre and Assiniboine people in north and central Montana. Father De Smet laid the foundation for missionary work among the these people when he baptized a Blackfoot chief and his family at St. Mary's Mission in 1841. De Smet did not extend missionary activity to Blackfoot country until 1846 when he and Father Nicholas Point traveled to their camps to explore the possibility of evangelizing among their people. Point wintered among the Blackfoot while De Smet traveled to St. Louis to report on the progress of western missions. After a winter of missionary work, Point left in the spring for Canada on orders from his superiors in Europe. After Father Point's departure from the Blackfoot camp, the people were only visited occasionally by priests traveling through their country. An attempt to establish a permanent mission started in 1859 when Reverend Father Nicholas Congiato, Superior of the Rocky Mountain missions, sent Father Adrien Hoeken. He built his mission on the banks of the Teton River. A year later he abandoned this site and moved the mission to the Sun River. The Jesuits once again abandoned their mission in 1865 because of Blackfoot hostility. In 1874 the Jesuits reopened St. Peter's Mission at Bird Tail Rock, near present day Cascade, Montana.

Bishop Brondel was acting on behalf of the Jesuit fathers when he invited the Ursulines to establish an extension of their foundation at St. Peter's. Evidently the Jesuits at St. Peter's needed the services of nuns to help build their educational programs. Mother Amadeus was reluctant to initiate a new program at St. Peter's when she was still trying to build a foundation and mother house in Miles City. But, when Mother Amadeus learned that the Cleveland Ursulines were trying to obtain passes to travel to Montana and establish themselves at St. Peter's, she feared that if the Toledo Ursulines did not move soon, they would lose their place at the mission.

At the end of October, 1884, Mother Amadeus and two postulants, Sisters Martha Geehan and Mary Magdalen Golden, arrived at St. Peter's to establish a school for girls. The two postulants were from Miles City, where they entered the Ursuline Order under the direction of Mother Amadeus. The mother superior left Sister Sacred Heart in charge of the Miles City convent and overseeing the construction of the Ursuline boarding school. Even though the sisters' financial resources were limited, Bishop Brondel believed the sisters were ready to contract the building of their school. He instructed Sister Sacred Heart "to put up a frame building immediately, according to the means at hand." Sister Sacred Heart made all the arrangements for a boarding school that consisted of "a house 30x40 ft. with a wing 24x30, and kitchen 12x16 attached; ten good large rooms."

Mother Amadeus' move from Miles City to St. Peter's was a permanent transfer. She left the sisters in Miles City to complete their plans to provide a boarding school for daughters of white settlers who lived in town and the surrounding area. She had already delivered Sisters Ignatius, Holy Angels, and Angela to the Cheyenne mission, which left Sisters St. Francis and Sacred Heart in Miles City. At St. Peter's, Mother Amadeus established a third house of the Toledo foundation that temporarily served the Blackfoot, Crow, and Gros Ventre-Assiniboine people. The Jesuits offered the Ursulines financial assistance in establishing their convent and school at St. Peter's Mission. The priests also bought the farm next to the mission and gave it to the sisters, along with two wagon horses, two milk cows, and $200 worth of provisions such as meat and flour. As a temporary school, the Jesuits rented their old house to the sisters, which had room for twenty children. The Jesuits eventually made a deal with the Ursulines that if the sisters could obtain more nuns from Toledo, then the fathers would pay the Ursulines $200 a year to teach the younger boys.

During the winter of 1884-1885, the Ursulines worked continuously to build and expand their educational program. Within two weeks of their arrival at the mission, they opened a school for the daughters of settlers who lived in the vicinity. By March, 1885, they established a school for Native American children with an enrollment of eleven Blackfoot girls. Father Eberschweiler, who was working among the Gros Ventre, increased the enrollment at the school when he sent "a wagonload of Indian girls" to the sisters.

The strain of planning and building at St. Peter's, plus the bitter cold of the Montana winter, weakened Mother Amadeus' immunity to disease and she caught pneumonia. Father Damiani, Superior of St. Peter's, gave Mother Amadeus a bed and relocated her to a "sheltered cabin that served as the sacristy."(Up to this time she evidently was sleeping on the floor of her small cabin.) This was a comforting place for Mother Amadeus. When the curtain partitioning her from the sanctuary was open, she could see the red light that burned outside the tabernacle, which housed the Blessed Sacrament. Father Damiani's concern for Mother Amadeus' worsening condition prompted him to summon the doctor from Fort Shaw and Mother Stanislaus from Toledo. The Toledo superior stayed with

Mother Amadeus and girls' art class. St. Peter's Mission. Courtesy of Jesuit Oregon Province Archives, Gonzaga University, Spokane.

Ursuline convent, St. Peter's Mission. Courtesy of Marquette University, Milwaukee.

Mother Amadeus and nursed her back to health. The ordeal convinced the mother superior that the Montana Ursulines should return with her to Toledo. Mother Amadeus refused this safe but unrewarding and unchallenging suggestion.

Accompanying Mother Stanislaus to Montana was Mary Fields, a black woman who worked at the Toledo convent. Mother Amadeus was one of Fields' favorite nuns. Her concern for Mother Amadeus' health compelled her to move to Montana where she could look after her and the other sisters. In Montana folklore, Fields is "Stagecoach Mary," one of the toughest women in Montana Territory. Descriptions of Fields often have it that "she was a tart-tongued, gun-toting, hard-drinking, cigar-and-pipe-smoking, 6-foot, 200 pound black woman who was tough enough to take on any two men."

After Mother Amadeus recovered from pneumonia, she found work for Fields as the mission freighter and in the mission laundry. The Jesuits, however, did not always appreciate Fields' explosive temper, especially when it placed her in situations where she did not demonstrate the qualities of refined womanhood. Bishop Brondel did not believe that Fields set a very good example for the children at the mission. He instructed the sisters to send her away. Unknown to the bishop, Mother Amadeus financed Fields in the restaurant business in nearby Cascade. The mother superior also asked the government to give Fields the mail route, which served the mission. Mother Amadeus' concern for Mary Fields superseded the bishop's ruling and her vow of obedience to superiors. In the Catholic hierarchy, the bishop was superior to all in his diocese. The sisters at St. Peter's, as well as the Jesuits, obeyed the instructions of the bishop. Mother Amadeus worked her way around the bishop's request and kept Fields very much in the sisters' lives.

The sisters also had to revise their vow to practice the rule of enclosure. If the sisters continued to practice it at all, it was certainly in a different form. Sister Mary of the Angels exemplified the changes in the sisters' communication with the outside world. It was Sister Mary's responsibility to play the organ at Sunday services. In so doing, the sister had to communicate and interact with the outside world. This seemed to place her in an awkward situation. She wrote, "I am organist at the Mission, and every Sunday perched on a stool surrounded by males and females--to me a strange position but, 'necessity knows no laws' until it is

Mary Fields (Stagecoach Mary). Courtesy of Ursuline Convent, Toledo.

removed and there I'll move with it. The soldiers are very kind to us, they were in last Sunday with a donation. On one occasion they came to church and, on leaving deposited on the organ while I am playing, from 25 to 50 cts. as their generosity prompts them. I am red before, but redder after ... there is such a simplicity out here that you can take all and everything as it comes."

Mother Amadeus' bout with pneumonia did not deter her from planning a building program to accommodate more students. From November, 1885 to May, 1887, the missionaries built six log structures to house and educate both Native American and white children. They financed their new structures from the tuition of white boarders and private donations. The settlers in the area supported the mission school for their children and donated time and money for its establishment. Until the Ursulines opened the girls' school, parents who chose a Catholic education for their children sent them to St. Vincent's Academy in Helena, a journey of more than twenty-four hours by stagecoach.

The schools at St. Peter's provided education for only a small percentage of Native American children from the Blackfoot, Crow, and Gros Ventre-Assiniboine Reservations. In 1885, Father Cataldo, Jesuit Superior of the Rocky Mountain missions, requested that BCIM ask permission from the Bureau of Indian Affairs to build missions on these reservations. The government granted Cataldo's request, which allowed the missionaries to expand their programs to educate and acculturate Native American children.

In September, 1887, Mother Amadeus prepared to open a school at the newly established St. Paul's Mission on the Gros Ventre-Assiniboine Reservation. The expansion of the Ursuline foundation to serve more Native American children, however, was difficult with so few sisters. Mother Amadeus wrote to the mother superior in Toledo of their efforts to prepare and outfit the new school. She told the mother superior, "I have made every endeavor to get all kinds of necessary garments ready for the future mission. We have eighty dresses, eighty skirts, one hundred and sixty chemises, one hundred and sixty aprons, shawls, stockings, etc." By September 14, 1887, they finished preparations and Mother Amadeus escorted two sisters to St. Paul's Mission on the Gros Ventre-Assiniboine Reservation.

The Atsina Indians, or, as traders called them, Gros Ventre, meaning big bellies, were the most northern division of the Arapaho. They were an Algonkian-speaking people who moved onto the Saskatchewan Plains in the eighteenth century. The Gros Ventre had a long association with the Blackfoot and most traders considered them part of the Blackfoot, confederacy. The Gros Ventre were traditional enemies of the Crees and Assiniboine, who forced the Gros Ventre into the Milk River area of north central Montana. The Judith Treaty of 1855 gave the Gros Ventre and Blackfoot common hunting grounds and an agency at Fort Benton. Subsequent treaties assigned the two nations joint occupation on the Fort Belknap Reservation.

The Assiniboine were the most northern tribe of the Siouian migration, who entered the Plains from the southeast. They were once allied with the Crees in the Hudson Bay trade, which gave them access to guns and metal utensils. The Crees and Assiniboine were principal middlemen in the fur trade, where they supplied Plains tribes with European material goods, including guns, in return for furs, cultivated vegetables, and native manufacturing. Most Plains people considered the Assinibione a poor nation because they owned few horses; the number of horses being an indicator of a person's or tribe's wealth. Ultimately, smallpox epidemics diminished the tribe's population, leaving only the very old and very young to continue tribal life, and, as with other Plains people, disease and the destructive forces inherent in the fur trade began to break down their traditional way of life and native culture. They made peace with the Gros Ventre around 1844. The two enjoyed a friendly trade relationship and by 1874, shared the same reservation.

Father Eberschweiler established St. Paul's Mission on the Fort Belknap Reservation in 1886. Under the guidelines of Grant's peace policy, the government promised the agency to the Methodists. The Methodists, however, did not establish a religious foundation among the Gros Ventre-Assiniboine. Seeking the opportunity to expand Catholic institutions in Montana, Father Eberschweiler petitioned President Grover Cleveland for permission to establish a Catholic mission on the Fort Belknap Reservation. Cleveland approved Eberschweiler's plan, and subsequently the Jesuit located the new mission in the Little Rockies, on a site that had good timber, agricultural land, and water. Eberschweiler spent the first winter at his log cabin mission learning the Assiniboine language and writing an

St. Paul's Mission, 1929. Courtesy of Marquette University, Milwaukee.

Indian Catechism. When the priest was able, he went to Fort Benton, the nearest supply depot some 200 miles away, to find a contractor and laborers to build a mission building that would house a boarding school for the children and provide quarters for the missionaries. By the fall of 1887, the mission was completed and Mother Amadeus and the Ursulines arrived to open their school.

Under the government contract system, it was necessary for the sisters to fill enrollment quotas in order to receive government appropriations, which helped to fund the school. But, it was often difficult for the sisters to maintain the level of enrollment they needed to sustain their institutions. In the first year of operation at St. Paul's, the sisters only enrolled eighteen children in the school. Low attendance stemmed from several factors. One was that parents generally did not trust the missionaries to care for their children. The sisters had to convince the parents that their children's future would be more secure if they acquired the education needed to live successfully in white society. Another factor that slowed enrollment was the anti-mission-school propaganda directed at the parents from non-Catholic government employees at the agency, which undermined the missionaries standing with the parents. Finally, the competition from the government's new educational policy for Native Americans also hampered the missionaries efforts. In the 1880s, the federal government devised a new policy that emphasized sending Native American children to off-reservation boarding schools. The point was to hasten the assimilation of Native American children into white culture. There was a new urgency because of western migration.

Americans preparing to move west in the 1880s demanded that the federal government open Indian lands. In response to the pressure from western migrants, the government devised a plan to break up tribal lands and assign an allotment in severalty to reservation Indians. Accordingly, the government stressed a new program, which taught Native Americans to be self-sufficient and take on the responsibilities of private ownership. The most efficient method implemented by the government to accomplish these civilization programs was the development of manual-labor schools. The idea was to send reservation children to schools like Carlisle in Pennsylvania, where children were completely removed from their culture; they would use the English language, develop a white work ethic, and become useful citizens.

The Catholic missionaries fought the manual labor school concept offered by the federal government. The missionaries did not base their objections solely on the enrollment numbers game, but more on the Catholic philosophy of Native American education. Unlike the government program, the religious believed that the natural educational path of Native Americans was from parent to child, not the other way around. Secular education, according to the Catholics, did not educate the "savage" parent, nor did it educate the child if the parent remained in a "savage" condition. The Catholic solution was Christianity; all people could be converted. To be converted was synonymous with being civilized. The thought was that, "the parent, transformed by religion into a morally civilized being, ceases to be an obstacle to the training of his children, while the educating of the children under the very eye of the parent, becomes, in turn, greatly beneficial to the parent himself."

The Department of the Interior could enforce government educational philosophy for contract schools only as long as the government paid the bill. As already mentioned, the government reduced appropriations in the 1890s and stopped funding altogether by 1900. Without government control, the missionaries were free to educate Native American children according to the Catholic concept of what constituted a civilized society. First and foremost, the Catholic missionaries taught Native American children to lead a Christian life directed toward the salvation of the soul. The sacraments and Christian instruction were the means of salvation. Thereafter, they were to help them develop the necessary skills to support a Christian family, expanding the moral and intellectual life of the Native American people.

Father Eberschweiler actively opposed government efforts to send Native American children to off-reservation boarding schools. With the same determination, government officials insisted that separation from their parents was the best educational route for Native American children. Both sides used the parents to obtain their goals. By coercing parents with lies about their children's welfare, government officials and the missionaries attempted to gain control over the education of native children. For example, both sides used intimidation in their campaign to win students. The representative from Carlisle accused the priest of threatening to excommunicate the parents if the did not send their children to the mission school. And the Catholics accused government officials of lying to the parents and threatening that if they did not willingly send their children to Carlisle, then the soldiers would take their children away and withhold their rations. He also told the parents that their children were sick and starving at the mission school and that the sisters disciplined them by sending them to jail.

Part of the missionaries' insistence that the children attend the mission school was their perception that the government provided little guidance in the moral well-being of the children and their families. It was particularly upsetting to the missionaries that the government did little to stop prostitution among young girls on the reservation. One way in which reservation families survived the meager rations offered by the government was to sell their daughters into prostitution. Father Eberschweiler first became aware of prostitution on the reservation in 1885. At that time, he claimed that the Indian agent withheld meat from the Indians and that "prostitution of most of the women was an another way of gaining some money from the post [Fort Belknap]." Even though the government tried to stop Native women from approaching the men at the fort, prostitution among the girls continued. In 1887, Father Eberschweiler maintained that parents also "sold their daughters for a horse or worse to traders." The sisters believed that the best way to provide a moral and religious atmosphere for the girls was to keep them at the boarding school and not even allow the girls to return to their homes during vacation periods.

The sisters' school among the Gros Ventre-Assiniboine was by their standards a success. The reluctance of the parents to send their children away from home was a common situation on all Montana reservations. But, generally the families on the Fort Belknap Reservation believed that industrial training provided at the mission school was a necessity for their children. The Indian people also accepted the tenets of Catholicism as they perceived them. The willingness of Native Americans to receive Catholicism motivated Mother Amadeus to realize her long-desired goal to establish a native sisterhood. At St. Paul's, the Ursulines began educating Native American girls to perform apostolic work among their own people. The missionaries considered the mission in the Little Rockies a success, and St. Paul's developed the reputation of being a place of tranquillity and peace. Mother Amadeus often left the mother house at St. Peter's to enjoy a retreat in the Little Rockies where she found "rest and spiritual joy."

The Ursulines' success in building their convents and schools always depended on obtaining financial resources. Neither the per capita allowance allocated to the missionaries from the federal government nor the tuition from boarders was sufficient to run their institutions at the different missions. If it was not for the generosity of Mother Katharine of the Sisters of the Blessed Sacrament, Mother Amadeus could not have continued expanding their convents and schools among Native people in Montana.

Mother Katharine was Katharine Drexel, heiress to the fortune of Francis Martin Drexel, a nineteenth-century financier and founder of Drexel and Company. Katharine's father, Francis Anthony Drexel, along with Anthony Joseph and Joseph William Drexel, continued to expand Drexel and Company into a world-wide investment house. After the death of Katharine's step-mother in 1883 and father in 1885, Katharine and her two sisters inherited most their parent's estate. The Drexel sisters had the same philanthropic concerns as their parents and gave generously to Catholic organizations that benefited the needy.

In 1885, Reverend Joseph Stephan, director of the BCIM, requested financial aid from the Drexel sisters to build Native American schools. This was the beginning of a long financial relationship between Katharine and the BCIM. The financial donations of Katharine Drexel allowed the

Catholics to expand mission schools on reservations throughout the West. In 1891, Katharine Drexel founded the Sisters of the Blessed Sacrament, an order that worked exclusively with Indian and Negro children.

Mother Amadeus contacted Katharine Drexel in 1888 to ask for money to build a structure at St. Peter's large enough to house a convent, novitiate, Indian school, and a school for "poor white children." She explained to Drexel,

> We have at present seven novices; twenty-five young women, hearing of our missionary work and burning with zeal for the conversion of souls, have volunteered to come out to help us; but to my distress I have been obliged to defer their entrance into the Novitiate until I could offer them a shelter. We have thirty Indian children and twenty 'white Indians', children of our hardy pioneers who know almost little about our Lord as the Indians themselves. We are seventy in number crowded into our lowly log-cabin convent.

Mother Amadeus contended that it was important to have a novitiate to train missionaries "to work for many missions in the Rocky Mountains" including an expansion of the Ursulines to Alaska. Mother Amadeus ended with a description of the nuns' life in Montana: "It is now thirty-six degrees below zero and fierce winds are driving the snow through the many crevices of our mud roof and the cracks in our daubed cabin walls. The floor is our bed and frequently we find our coverlets a downy fleece of snow in the morning." Drexel promised Mother Amadeus $5,000 toward the new convent.

After the BCIM granted Father Cataldo permission to establish a mission on the Blackfoot Reservation, the missionaries approached Katharine Drexel for a donation to build Holy Family Mission.

Mother Katharine took the Jesuit's request under advisement but she was concerned that the priests owned the properties on which she would finance the building of permanent structures. In 1887, Chief White Calf gave the Jesuits land on Two Medicine Creek for a school. If Drexel donated the money to build the school, all the property would belong to the Jesuits. Katharine Drexel refused to donate more money until the Jesuits signed an agreement indicating that the missions would be "preserved in perpetuity to the Indians. They are surrounded by so many greedy whites that it seems necessary to protect them." She was not necessarily accusing the Jesuits of being greedy. Her concern was that if the whites forced Native Americans off their lands, then the Jesuits might continue to minister to whites and not Native people.

In negotiating with the Jesuits, Drexel demonstrated her ability as a businesswoman and guaranteed that the fathers would not gain financial control of the missions. She agreed to send the Jesuits $14,000 for Holy Family Mission once they signed her agreement. She would provide the money in two installments. The Jesuits were to keep receipts and written debits and credits. Before they could spend completely the $7,000, they had to send the receipts to the BCIM. If the financial accounting was to her satisfaction, she would allocate the remaining $7,000 with the condition that all receipts be sent to the BCIM. Holy Family formally opened in 1890 when father Damiani and three Ursulines from St. Peter's arrived at the mission. Mother Amadeus sent Mother Angela Lincoln as superior of Holy Family along with Sisters Irene Arvin and Monica Martin.

The Catholics established Holy Family to serve the Blackfoot people who resided in north-central Montana. The Blackfoot nation is actually a confederacy consisting of three tribes known as the Blackfoot, Piegan, and Blood. Because they share the same cultural traits, customs, and language, whites referred to them collectively as Blackfoot. It is believed that the origin of their name stems from the black soles of their moccasins, which were evidently blackened from soil around where they once lived. The Blackfoot have few legends that indicate where they lived before whites encountered them on the Northern Plains in the early eighteenth century. At that time, they occupied an area from the North Saskatchewan River in Canada to the Missouri River in Montana. From information gathered by whites who lived among them for periods of time, their original homelands were in wooded areas of the Northeast.

The same year that Holy Family opened, the federal government started to reduce appropriations for contract schools. Senator Thomas H. Carter of Montana, however, introduced a bill that continued federal funds to support the school at Holy Family. The government appropriated funds for one hundred students at the mission's boarding school. The sisters at the mission school at Holy Family suffered the same difficulties as other

Catholic missions in convincing Native parents to relinquish their children to the missionaries. The missionaries were sympathetic to the concerns of the parents. One wrote, "Who has not heard of the extreme fondness of the Indian for his offspring? To tear the child away from his parent is like inflicting a deep wound in the Indian heart while to punish the child by corporal punishment is almost an outrage on the parent."

The missionaries also understood the children's hesitancy in accepting life in a boarding school.

> The children's reluctance will not be hard to understand when we remember how deeply rooted in the Indian child is his love of home and of the freedom of the plains--Here especially where an Indian is seldom seen going afoot, it is no little sacrifice for the Indian child to be deprived for an entire year of his pony and saddle. Add to this the strange feeling of having to lead a totally different life amidst strange people and one may easily understand the timidity bordering on fright which takes hold of an Indian child on first entering the school.

To fill the school to capacity, the missionaries drove their wagon into the mountains to collect Native American children. One person's account explained, "went up mountain in a wagon, returned in the night with one school boy. After sunset, boy began to cry, and cried on till we came to school." Once missionaries found children for the school, they had a struggle keeping them there. It was especially difficult in the spring when they went on picnics. At such occasions, there was always the possibility that some would take the opportunity to flee. When students left without permission, the sisters went in the mission wagon to bring them back. They believed that the desire for freedom was part of the Indian nature. Frequent runaways earned severe punishments. The missionaries publicly whipped children and expelled those identified as leaders of runaways.

Like the Sisters of Providence at St. Ignatius, the Ursulines at Holy Family educated the young girls in their boarding school to the customs of nineteenth-century Victorian culture, which emphasized the virtues of "refined womanhood." It was the Ursulines' responsibility to transform

Native American girls into middle-class white women who would impart the culturally accepted values of white society.

Unlike the Flathead woman, whom was respected because of her work and contribution to the tribe, a Blackfoot woman's life was one of hard work and little reward. Her responsibilities included rearing her children and taking care of the needs of the family such as meals, clothing, and housing. She also dressed buffalo hides and made domestic tools and utensils. When it was time to move, she packed the camp and moved it herself. Before the aid of horses eased their efforts, Blackfoot women packed their belongings on travois, which were pulled by dogs. When a woman became too old to have the strength to perform her duties, her people abandoned her and she faced certain death alone. Parents educated their children to undertake male and female responsibilities. Women taught their daughters the skills that would make them attractive wives, such as how to dress hides, prepare food, make clothing, and build lodges. Fathers taught their sons skills that would make them good hunters and warriors.

The sisters began cultural transformation of Blackfoot children by removing material possessions and changing cultural habits to conform to accepted standards of white behavior. This meant changing living habits that were inherent to Native American life. One sister explained that, "The families then lived in tepees and were accustomed to sleeping on buffalo skins, to eating with their fingers, and to moving the entire home when a site became too filthy." The sisters taught the girls to accept living in permanent wooden structures, sleeping on beds, and using "good" table manners in the dining room.

In 1890, the missionaries located Holy Family Mission below a hundred-foot sandstone cliff on the banks of Two Medicine River. The cliff protected the mission from severe north winds but not from cold temperatures. Every morning the sisters were up early, lighting forty stoves in their building and thawing the water in the basins. By then, the Ursulines had labored six years among the Native American people. They still embraced their altruistic goals as women religious, but they no longer expected to maintain an enclosed or traditional life style. Life as they knew it in their Toledo convent could not be duplicated in the frontier environment. They experienced a truly impoverished life as they devoted themselves to the salvation of souls. This was especially true of the sisters who Mother Amadeus sent to establish a mission among the Cheyennes.

Within the photograph: OLD CATHOLIC MISSION — TONGUE RIVER MONTANA

COPYRIGHT 1903 BY L.A. HUFFMAN

Ursuline nuns by first convent at St. Joseph Labre Mission. Jesuit Oregon Province Archives.

5

THE TRAIL TO
ST LABRE'S

Mother Amadeus escorted Sisters Sacred Heart, Ignatius, and St. Angela to the newly established mission among the Cheyenne in March, 1884, three months after they arrived in Miles City. The mission consisted of a log cabin on an old homestead purchased by Father Eyler. He bought the property in February from Thomas Cook for $600. The humble beginnings of this mission amongst the poorest of the Plains tribes prompted Bishop Brondel to name the new foundation after St. Joseph Labre, the beggar Saint who was "poorest of God's poor." The sisters who went to St. Labre's Mission faced difficult challenges in developing their school among the Cheyenne. They suffered along with the Cheyenne people from inadequate food and very few material comforts. But perhaps more upsetting were the periods of isolation and loneliness without the spiritual guidance of a priest. For the first eighteen months of their missionary life among the Cheyenne, the sisters were alone at St. Labre's Mission. This was an unexpected situation that placed the sisters in a position where they had to assume the ministerial responsibilities of a priest in addition to fulfilling their own duties to educate Cheyenne children.

After tending to the spiritual and physical needs of the Cheyenne people for over a year, the Jesuits relieved some of the sisters' missionary responsibilities by appointing Father Aloysius Van Der Velden to the mission post in October, 1885. Father Van Der Velden worked with the Ursulines for twelve years. During that time, the two religious orders realized few successes in their attempt to teach the Cheyenne people the dictates of white culture and the tenets of Catholicism. Part of the missionaries' failure can be attributed to their lack of knowledge concerning Native American life. They judged Cheyenne culture according to their understanding of what constituted a civilized society. Ultimately, this prevented them from understanding the needs of the Cheyenne people. Their lack of success also can be credited to the federal government's Indian policy for the Northern Cheyenne Reservation, which contributed to the impoverished condition of the Cheyenne people. This, along with the settlement of white ranchers onto reservation land along the Tongue River, threatened Cheyenne existence. To fight against poverty and white encroachment into their territory, the Cheyenne used the only means available to them; they continued Native traditions, especially religious practices, which strengthened their culture and renewed their faith that they would again control their destiny.

Correspondence among the Ursulines at St. Labre, Miles City, and Toledo provides information about the sisters' isolation at the Cheyenne mission and the nature of their work with the people. Their letters, however, do not relate the dire condition of the Cheyenne or the general dissatisfaction the people had with reservation life. Father Van Der Velden, on the other hand, wrote candidly about his impressions of the Cheyenne and the conflicts between the federal government, the white settlers, and the Cheyenne over settlement in the Tongue River Valley. Through the letters of the Ursuline Nuns and Father Van Der Velden, one gains insight into missionary life and the hostile environment in which the Catholics tried to change Native American culture.

An Executive Order in November, 1884, established the 371,000 acre Northern Cheyenne Reservation. The reservation was the culmination of years of struggle by the Cheyenne to inhabit an area in the northern Plains that they considered part of their traditional homeland. The Cheyenne fought with other Plains Indians and with whites who crossed the Plains in the 1840s and 1850s, over intrusion and settlement in Cheyenne Territory. Native American hostility to white settlement on Indian lands prompted the United States government to confine the Plains Indians to reservations. In the Fort Wise treaty of 1861, the government negotiated a settlement in which the Cheyenne agreed to a reservation on the Arkansas River in the Southern Plains. The northern band of the Cheyenne, however, refused to accept the treaty; they did not want to move from their northern hunting grounds.

In 1876, the United States army waged an active campaign to force the Sioux and Northern Cheyenne-Arapaho onto reservations. The outcome of this struggle was a battle between Sioux-Cheyenne forces and the United States Seventh Cavalry under the command of General George Armstrong Custer. Custer's defeat only encouraged the United States Army to settle quickly the "Indian problem." By the summer of 1877, General Nelson A. Miles captured and sent 1,000 Northern Cheyenne to join their kinsmen on the reservation in Indian Territory in the present state of Oklahoma. The Northern Cheyenne were not able to acclimate to southern reservation life. In September, 1887, over 300 men, women, and children escaped from Indian Territory and fought their way north to their homeland. The army captured the Cheyenne and imprisoned them at Fort Robinson in Nebraska. At Fort Robinson, the army refused the Cheyenne food, water, and fuel until they agreed to return south. Their answer was another escape in January. The army finally subdued the Cheyenne and removed them to Fort Keogh, Montana. The Cheyenne won their battle to stay in the North.

In Montana, General Miles enlisted Northern Cheyenne as scouts to help capture recalcitrant Native Americans with the promise, that when all was peaceful, he would help the Cheyenne choose a reservation to their liking. While at Fort Keogh, the Cheyenne hunted in the Tongue and Powder River areas, where there were few white settlers but a sufficient amount of game, fresh water, timber, and range. They chose this region for their reservation.

White settlement along the Tongue, Rosebud, and Powder Rivers occurred shortly after the Cheyenne selected this area for their future home. Increased settlement reduced the wildlife population in the region, especially the buffalo. In a matter of only a few years, white hunters eliminated almost all the buffalo from the Tongue River area. For example, in 1878, residents of Miles City commented on the large herds of buffalo grazing near the city. One young woman observed "We saw the hills black with buffalo on the north side, even coming down to the foot of Main Street." Only two years later a cattleman stated that:

from the Porcupine [River] clear to Miles City the bottoms are liberally sprinkled with the carcasses of dead buffalo. In many places they lie thick on the ground, fat and the meat not yet spoiled, all murdered for their hides which are piled like cord wood all along the way. Probably ten thousand have been killed in this vicinity this winter. Slaughtering the buffalo is a government measure to subjugate the Indians.

Cheyenne material culture centered on the buffalo; the people relied upon the animal for food, shelter, dress, and weapons. Without a sufficient supply of buffalo in Cheyenne territory, it was difficult for the people to maintain their traditional way of life. Also detrimental to cultural survival was the influx of white settlers into Cheyenne hunting areas. With the buffalo off the range, Texas cattlemen began moving their cattle up the Texas trail to graze along the Tongue and Rosebud Rivers in 1883. By October of that year, there were 600,000 Texas cattle competing for range grass. Along with the big cattle companies, smaller outfits also settled along the Tongue and Rosebud Rivers.

In 1884, two cultures converged along the Tongue River, where both tried to maintain their way of life by occupying the land. White settlers were looking for range on which to graze more cattle and resented the occupation of land by the Cheyenne. Some settlers built homesteads and grazed cattle on land rightfully belonging to the Cheyenne people. Evidently the Executive Order of 1884, which established the Cheyenne Reservation, did not provide for a land survey. Without boundary lines, white settlers were free to move into Cheyenne Territory. While the settlers were enjoying the benefits of the Cheyenne's' land, the Indian people were without the means with which to support themselves. It was within this potentially combative environment that the Ursulines prepared to leave Miles City for St. Labre's Mission in the spring of 1884. It is doubtful, however, when the Jesuits made their plans to open a mission among the Cheyenne, that they were aware of the antagonism between Indian and white in the Tongue River Valley. If they were cognizant of the growing hostility, it did not stop them from sending three women to an isolated mission outpost. The immediate concern seemed to be whether the sisters obeyed their religious obligations. For example, Father Lindesmith from

Fort Keogh took charge of the sisters' trip to the mission by arranging for the soldiers from the fort to escort the women to the Cheyenne Reservation. The Reverend Father evidently assumed that the sisters needed special instructions concerning their religious deportment and their physical care. He instructed the Ursulines that, while under the care of the soldiers, they did not have to follow their religious customs such as fasting and offering routine prayers. Instead he encouraged them to partake of the soldiers' camp cooking, which would provide the Ursulines with the necessary nutrition to endure the arduous trip to the mission. Lindesmith advised, "The soldiers will cook a little something for you, and they have meat three times a day, and you must take it too, so that you can stand the journey." The sisters did as Lindesmith instructed. But, the women were resourceful and had provided for their own needs. As Sister Ignatius expressed, "We had packed a lunch in our hampers but as we were ordered, we ate what the soldiers had prepared." Their trip to the mission took three days. They traveled by army ambulance along a road that wound through buttes and over rugged terrain. Each night the men set up camp while the sisters waited in the ambulance. The soldiers then cooked dinner that consisted of bacon, potatoes, and coffee. The next morning the soldiers served the same meal for breakfast.

The sisters arrived at the Cheyenne mission four days after leaving Miles City. Their new convent home consisted of a three-room log structure with a mud roof and dirt floors. The rooms were only accessible from the outside. The sisters occupied the largest room, which was 16x22 feet. They decided to use the middle room as a classroom, and the third room was Father Eyler's quarters. Cowboys employed by the previous owner had lived in the cabin before the sisters. They left the walls covered with the *Police Gazette* and an assortment of benches and dry goods boxes. It pleased the sisters to inherit this odd assortment of furniture. The soldiers helped the sisters settle into their new home by clearing a path to the river so that the women could easily carry their water. The men also chopped wood, fixed the stove, and helped the sisters to construct an altar, a kitchen table, and some stools. The sisters improvised with the few materials available to make their convent comfortable. They used the crate from the organ they brought with them from Miles City as a cupboard for china and tinware. They also constructed the altar at one end of their room and covered the ceiling and back of the altar with muslin. The sisters made a calico curtain for the sanctuary and placed the Blessed Sacrament in the tabernacle near the altar. It was early morning the following day before the sisters finished preparations for their convent, school, and church. With the work completed, the soldiers returned to Fort Keogh. Two days later White Bull and his daughter, Yellow Stocking, escorted Mother Amadeus back to Miles City.

Two months later Father Eyler left the mission. When the sisters arrived, they noticed that he had lost considerable weight while staying at the mission alone. By June health problems brought on by the harsh environment convinced him he needed to return to Ohio. For the first eighteen months, the sisters were alone at the mission. Evidently, it was difficult to secure a permanent priest who could withstand the hardships of primitive life among the Cheyenne. The sisters, however, had the faith, the strength, and the endurance to withstand the austerity of mission life. The fathers later recognized their tenacity. One wrote,

> After the fathers started the mission, the sisters were left quite alone for more than six months. Bishop Brondel visited them once or twice to keep up their courage in their hard circumstances. Poor Sisters! No Communion, No Mass, No Confession. Alone amongst wild Indians who knew nothing about God or religion ... I admire your courage. If the Old Testament had its heroic women, the new testament has its heroines two [sic].

The sisters organized the school for Cheyenne children shortly after arriving at the mission in April. By summer, 1884, they had forty students. Along with establishing an educational program for the children, the sisters offered them two meals a day, breakfast and dinner. Their resources were limited; the best they could offer the children was fat bacon and flour mixed with corn meal. They augmented this meager diet by planting a garden from which they dried fruits and vegetables for the winter. Planting and harvesting their garden, however, was a difficult task without the extra labor provided by the priest.

After Father Eyler left, the Jesuits appointed Father Barcelo to the mission. He lasted for six weeks. During his short tenure, he helped the sisters "in the garden ... mowing of the hay, the digging of the cellar, the well, chopped the wood, etc." When he left in September, the sisters were on their own to maintain the mission and secure their own food. The Cheyenne seemed to understand the sisters' difficult situation in maintaining the mission without the help of a priest. Sister Ignatius wrote:

> It would touch you to see their kindness to us, the morning of Rev. Father Barcelo's departure. They saw we felt bad, and did everything to help us. Were it not for our dear boys, we would have a hard time with the horses and wood, etc.

Father Barcelo left the Cheyenne Reservation in fear for his life after a threatening incident between George Yoakum, a retired soldier from Fort Keogh, and white settlers from the mission vicinity. While Yoakum was under General Miles' command, he helped settle the Northern Cheyenne along the Tongue River and was influential in convincing Bishop Brondel that the Cheyenne could benefit from missionary teachings. The settlers in the area did not want the Catholics influencing the Cheyenne because the missionaries interfered with white efforts to force the Indians from desirable lands. Because Yoakum helped the Cheyenne and the missionaries, settlers considered him an enemy. Men, referred to by the sisters as cowboys, found Yoakum in Father Barcelo's room one night. They dragged him several miles from the mission where they "scourged him most unmercifully till they extorted from him a promise that he would leave the country." When Barcelo tried to defend Yoakum, one of the men "placed a revolver,' a six shooter, on his forehead and said if he moved they would shoot." Evidently Yoakum left the country and Father Barcelo escaped to Miles City. Mother Amadeus reported that "he [Barcelo] came to us here all bothered and bruised and torn."

Mother Amadeus worried about the sisters' safety after Barcelo and Yoakum left the mission. She stated that, "I always feel much disquieted when they are alone at St. Labre--my fear arises from a dread of the white Indians, not from the dear Cheyenne." Barcelo left the mission under the pretense of bad health, and the sisters expected that he would return when he recovered. While the sisters awaited Barcelo's return, they endured the harsh winter of 1885, during which temperatures often fell to 30 or 40 degrees below zero. Sister Ignatius commented, "We hear that some cattle were frozen last night, and by the feeling of our room this morning at 4 o'clock and the looks of our door, we concluded it must have been a very cold night." Luckily, before they left Toledo, Mother Stanislaus had outfitted them with warm clothing.

The sisters spent the winter learning the Cheyenne language and teaching the children. One of the biggest obstacles for them to overcome if they were to educate and acculturate the Cheyenne children was that of language. Along with serving the children meals and teaching them how to sew and play games, the sisters taught the children the English language while learning the Cheyenne language. They also instructed the children "how to spell and read and count and write, and above all, hear them say, "'My God, I give thee my heart,' and the 'Our father,' and 'Hail Mary,' Creed, and a good part of the 'Little Catechism.'"

The sisters were physically and spiritually isolated on the Cheyenne reservation. They could, perhaps, provide for their physical comfort, but the essential part of their religious culture relied on a priest to minister to them the sacraments of their faith. It was especially difficult for the sisters during the Christmas season. On Christmas Eve they did not celebrate Mass as usual. Their only consolation to their spiritual privation was that they had the Blessed Sacrament, which to them meant they were not alone, for Christ was with them.

> On Christmas day, the sisters took over the role of the priest and planned church service for the Cheyenne. One sisters wrote, "Our Holy Angels has been practicing the Christmas hymns, and our Angela is fixing our little altar; we are going to assist at 'Spiritual Mass', and have all our hymns at 12 o'clock tonight. We are going to make it Christmas, Mother, as much as we can without our dear Jesuit, and tomorrow, Mother, our dear children will say for the first time, the Rosary, or rather Beads, all in Cheyenne .

All of January the sisters anticipated Father Barcelo's return. "We are still alone every day expecting to see our saintly Jesuit's return and every day disappointed." They continued their daily routine and religious observances as usual. "Our Order of the day is exactly as is marked in our 'Constitutions.' Now, alas, we have no Mass at 7 o'clock, but at that hour we assist at Holy Mass spiritually, and afterwards take our 'piece of bread.' We try to keep our holy Rule as perfectly as is possible."

The sisters developed a daily routine of religious exercises, language study, and teaching. By the following summer, they altered this schedule to accommodate the warmer weather. In the cool of the morning and evening, they worked in the fields tending their gardens. They divided the rest of their day between prayer, household chores, teaching school, and language studies. They also supplied food to the children and visited the sick.

Without the help of a priest at the mission, the responsibility of caring for the spiritual life of the Cheyenne people belonged to the sisters. As missionaries, it was their duty to convince the Cheyenne to give up traditional religious customs, particularly those that offended Christian beliefs. The sisters, however, found it difficult to stop the Cheyenne from practicing many of their traditional ways. In particular, the sisters noted that it was impossible for them to change Cheyenne burial customs, which dictated that the people bury their dead immediately in a location far removed from their camp. They feared that the ghost of the departed might stay around the body and carry away the spirit of the living. It was also the practice after the death of a child for relatives to cut the child's hair, gash the heads and the calves of the legs with knives, and cut off the tip of one of the fingers. They also did not wash off the dried blood for a long period of time.

The sisters witnessed this ritual in several variations. After the death of a ten-year-old boy, the Cheyenne buried him in the distant hills. It horrified the sisters when they saw the parents the next morning. According to Sister St. Angela,

> Their hair hung loosely over their eyes. The man was wrapped in a white sheet. The woman was dressed but wrapped in an old white rag. One of her fingers was cut off at the first joint. Her arms and legs had been slashed with a sharp knife and were still bleeding. For one year they never washed in the river.

In a similar incident, when the sisters participated in the funeral procession of a little girl, they noticed the child's mother sharpening her knife. Knowing that she intended to slash her calves and cut off her finger, the sisters tried to reason with the woman that self mutilation was not necessary. The missionaries thought they had succeeded when the mother promised she would not use her knife. The next day when the sisters saw the mother, however, her legs were bleeding and she would not let them tend to the wounds, believing that the blood needed to dry and fall off. Death customs eventually gave way as the Cheyenne adopted missionary teachings. Sister St. Angela again wrote that, "It took many years for the priest to show them that God did not like this."

After Father Van Der Velden arrived at St. Labre's in October, 1885, he assumed many of the duties the sisters had performed during their period of religious isolation at the mission. From the beginning of his tenure, Van Der Velden realized that his work to convert the Cheyenne would be a difficult task. He wrote to his father in Holland explaining the unfavorable circumstances under which he would begin his missionary duties.

> The distribution of prizes took place yesterday ... I received the highest distinction that of the most dangerous, rather let me say, the most difficult post. It is the most difficult of all the missions in charge for the society. I have a new mission by the Cheyenne, as yet a real Indian wild people, which for two years ... was cruelly treated by the soldiers, but chose to be shot dead-man after man, rather than to be driven back off the ground of their forefathers.

Van Der Velden was a newly ordained priest when the Jesuits sent him to St. Labre's Mission. Like the sisters, a missionary's life appealed to him because he believed that guiding the Indian soul to heaven was serving God in the most worthy manner; and, as a good religious, he needed to experience sacrifices he believed inherent to mission life. He wrote to his father, "without little sacrifices one can never be a good religious, with them never a bad religious, and what does it matter to live a few years less conveniently, when one keeps before ones eyes the salvation of souls and heaven. I will merit a better place in heaven here where I am, than I would

St. Joseph Labre Mission. Courtesy of Jesuit Oregon Province Archive, Gonzaga University, Spokane.

have ever merited in Europe." Shortly after arriving at the mission, Father Van Der Velden, along with Father Peter Prando, S.J., who helped Van Der Velden for a period of time, made the rounds of Indian lodges. Their purpose was to become acquainted with the Cheyenne people and to gain their trust. The Jesuits' first visit was to the lodge of a man Van Der Velden called "emancipated" because his home was made of logs. When Van Der Velden entered the lodge there were nine men seated on beds, which the Cheyenne positioned along the walls. He recited to the men a phrase that he had memorized for the occasion. "To see you makes me glad, for I love all the Cheyenne."

The Cheyenne reacted to the Catholics' overture of friendliness by including the priests in their traditional pipe-smoking ceremony. This ceremony was important in Cheyenne culture and had various meanings. For example, it was customary to smoke the pipe when guests entered a man's lodge. The ceremony had a religious connotation; before the host offered the pipe to his guests, he prayed and pointed the pipestem to the spirit of the sky, the spirit of the ground, and the spirits who lived in four different directions. In Cheyenne religious culture, people believed in one Supreme Being or Maheo, the All Father. Four Sacred Persons reigned under Maheo and lived at the four different points of the universe. The four spirits represented all elements of the universe--the sun, moon, stars, and lesser Powers who assume animal forms. In the pipe-smoking ritual, the host prayed for goodwill from All Father and the spirits. It was customary for the Cheyenne to smoke at important events; the priests' visit was such an occasion.

The Jesuits no doubt knew of the religious significance of the pipe smoking ceremony. Since Jesuit contact with eastern Native Americans in the 1600s, the priests recognized that Native American customs could be adapted as a vehicle to teach Christianity. The priests took advantage of occasions when people gathered for ceremonial or tribal business to teach Christian doctrine. The priests outwardly accepted the sacred meaning implied in the pipe smoking ceremony because it facilitated their missionary goals. On the Cheyenne Reservation, it was important for Fathers Van Der Velden and Prando to establish that they respected Cheyenne customs. It was the first step toward winning the peoples' confidence and, hopefully, their souls.

It was a difficult task, however, for Van Der Velden to accommodate himself to the Cheyenne way of life because so much of it was different from his culture's ways. This was apparent from his first visit with the Cheyenne people. When recalling the pipe smoking ceremony Van Der Velden commented,

> The pipe now makes the rounds, after having been lit by
> the head of the family. Four or five already had the pipe
> in their mouth when it was my turn. What was to be done.
> To pass it up to the next one without smoking would be
> an insult. I overcame ... took a dozen puffs and passed the
> pipe to the next one. It is the first step which costs.

The sisters, too, had difficulty in working with Cheyenne children. The sisters, evidently were aware of their own uncharitable feelings and reasoned that they could overcome their displeasure by invoking God's love. One Ursuline Nun wrote that, through God's eyes, "It is all sweet, earnest work; all repugnance vanishes, for God sees and loves it. Formerly I could not have touched with my lips a cup from which another had drunk, or slept in a bed which I had found unkempt." The cultural clash between the missionaries and the Cheyenne impeded their mission to bring Catholic Christianity to the Cheyenne People. This was especially seen in their view of Cheyenne women. The missionaries judged men and women according to Victorian society's perception of men's and women's separate roles. In Victorian America, men assumed authority over their families and the world at large. For this reason, perhaps, Van Der Velden was more comfortable among Cheyenne men than he was among Cheyenne women. He admired the men whom, he considered fine "specimens" of manhood. He viewed the women, however, as "not only homely, but most of them absolutely abominable. I think our Dear Lord at the last day will have a fine time to make something decent out of them, because if He does not, everyone else will run out when they come in."

Van Der Velden, especially, did not like the strong influence that women had over Cheyenne men; it was his opinion that Cheyenne women kept men from going to Church services. The priest believed that Fire Crow's wife kept her husband from going to service by taking away his socks and moccasins; so if he attended church, he would have to walk barefoot on the frozen ground. It was also Van Der Velden's opinion that women angered easily. "If anybody should be astonished that a woman be able to rule a strong fellow, he must know that a mad Indian squaw is worse to fight than any person or animal whatsoever. She is a fury in the full sense of the word." Van Der Velden experienced this first-hand when he went to the lodges to evangelize. In one lodge, the priest started to tell a woman about the way to heaven. She interrupted him and asked, "Do you have meat?" The answer was "no." Her reply was, "We do not want your prayers they do not fill our stomachs." She then ran Van Der Velden out of the lodge with a burning stick from the fire. In another home, a woman ran after the priest with a knife. He reported that "he ran for dear life lucky his young legs outdistanced hers." Van Der Velden admitted that he "could handle the men but not the women, nobody could not even the chiefs."

The Ursulines also judged men and women in Cheyenne society according to the gender roles prescribed by Victorian Americans. The sisters had an opportunity to meet and observe the Cheyenne during their move from Miles City to the mission. During the caravan's second overnight stop, they camped along side a party of Cheyenne. While the soldiers prepared the sisters' camp, the nuns were especially observant of how the soldiers treated them in comparison to how Indian men treated Cheyenne women. The sisters looked on as the women unpacked and set up their tents while the men watched from the hillside. Sister Ignatius commented,

> It was a painful sight to see these great strong men lazily stretch themselves upon the grass while the squaws, some of them with papooses on their backs and others clinging to their sides perform all the labor, unload the ponies, pitch tents, chop and carry wood, build the fire, etc. A strange contrast indeed in this lonely spot in the wilderness between civilization and barbarity, Christianity and heathenism. In one camp, the woman, a degraded slave, in the other, every honorable and refining care lavished on her.

By European standards, most women did not assume labor intensive work such as the nuns witnessed of Cheyenne women. In Cheyenne society, however, the women were performing their usual role within the tribe, which they assumed with a certain amount of authority. They acquired this authority from their economic status and position in Cheyenne society, which depended on their acceptance into women's guilds. Guilds controlled the making of tipi covers and quill and bead designs for parfleches, dresses, and moccasins. In order for a woman to be accepted into a particular guild, she had to prepare elaborate feasts and bestow presents on the guild leader. Once in a guild, she learned the details of the art, the technical terms, and the symbolism of the design. Women also held status in their society in their role as mothers; they gave the Cheyenne future warriors.

Compared with some other Plains Indian women, Cheyenne women believed in chastity and, therefore, appeared very moral to white observers. Before marriage, they wore at all times a chastity rope that was wound around their legs. Evidently, the missionaries recognized the modesty of Cheyenne women. They commented that when they crossed a river, they would not lift their dresses or take off any of their clothing. There were also very few cases of adultery. If a man raped a Cheyenne woman, women of the tribe settled the matter. After the rape of one woman, who was accosted by a medicine man while attending to her child, the woman, along with several of her companions, found the aggressor. They cornered

Cheyenne women. St. Labre's Mission. Courtesy of Marquette University, Milwaukee.

Cheyenne Medicine Man. St.Labre's Mission. Courtesy of Marquette University, Milwaukee.

him alone on a hill, where they jumped him, dragged him by the hair, and hit his head with stones. They made him pay a horse and two blankets for his actions. He also received the condemnation of the whole tribe. Women, then, were the backbone of the Cheyenne community in that they shared a valuable role in providing economically for their people and in maintaining their cultural standards.

Generally, the missionaries did not view the Cheyenne as industrious people. In fact, they thought them to be "so lazy, that I doubt whether the devil wants them in hell, for they are too lazy to burn." What the sisters and Father Van Der Velden did not see was that the Cheyenne were not necessarily lazy but, perhaps, disillusioned with reservation life. Although transforming the Cheyenne into yeoman farmers was the desired goal of federal officials, the government did not supply the Cheyenne with suitable farming equipment, nor did they consider that the Cheyenne Reservation lacked sufficient water for agriculture. Whites occupied the areas of the reservation that did have water. The Cheyenne, therefore, did not always have the means with which to be industrious. Not only was it difficult for the Cheyenne to plant and harvest gardens, they also suffered from a lack of government rations. The missionaries claimed that the Indian agent often sold the rations promised by the federal government to the Cheyenne people. Mother Amadeus, contended that it was common knowledge in Miles City that the agent "cleared between fifty and sixty thousand dollars in two years by selling to outside parties the provisions sent on here for the Indians."

In November, 1885, the missionaries held a council with the Cheyenne chiefs to hear their grievances concerning reservation life. At the meeting the Cheyenne expressed their complaints against the Indian agent for not distributing sufficient rations and related how the people were starving. According to one Cheyenne,

> Last winter four of our women died of hunger; this winter we shall all die. You told us to cultivate the land, but we have no tools. We used to live on the buffalo; all the buffalo are now exterminated, and last winter all the antelope were killed. Some of us had cattle, but they were stolen from us. Winter is coming and we have no blankets.

The next day several Cheyenne men told Bishop Brondel, who was visiting from the diocese in Helena, that they had not eaten in four days. As an immediate response to the Cheyenne' hunger, the bishop bought a steer from the postmaster in Birney for $60 and divided it among twenty-nine families.

The Cheyenne believed that they could better their physical condition if they received promised rations from the government, and according to Father Van Der Velden, they viewed him as a means toward this end. Van Der Velden, however, considered it more important to improve the Cheyenne's spiritual condition. The priest had no intention of opening arbitration with the federal government, but he pretended to do so in order to manipulate the people into listening to his instructions. Evidently, Van Der Velden was upset with the Cheyenne because they walked out during his instruction of Catholic doctrine. When he asked them why they left his lectures, the Cheyennes told Van Der Velden that "the blackrobe speak badly." Van Der Velden interpreted this to mean that he was teaching them things they did not want to hear. The priest believed that the only way he could make the Cheyenne listen to him was to deceive them by offering to help with their requests to the federal government. Van Der Velden wrote that, "They promised to do all what I tell them on condition that I will say a strong 'good word' at Washington. Often then I must play a comedy on such occasions and I take a very big sheet of paper and keeping a serious face I write down all they tell me. This paper must then be sent to Washington-but the mailbox is the stove." Van Der Velden believed that his theatrics were necessary if he were to accomplish his missionary goals. The Cheyennes, however, became impatient with the priest for not understanding that they had more immediate concerns than listening to the Jesuit's lectures. They told Van Der Velden that since they did not receive from the Catholics what they expected, then they could do without the missionaries.

While Van Der Velden was trying to trick the Cheyenne into learning the beliefs of Catholicism, the Ursulines were trying to increase the number of students attending the boarding school. In keeping with Catholic educational philosophy, the missionaries believed that it was important to educate and convert Cheyenne children in order to reach the parents. According to one sister, the parents of Cheyenne children are "enraptured and ready to be converted" if their children "can sing or speak English, pray or make the Sign of the Cross. The only thing to do is to take the children and train them; then the elders fall in readily."

Without adequate assistance from the federal government or the missionaries, the Cheyenne had little incentive to change their way of life. Perhaps, if anything, white indifference to the Cheyenne's material needs only reinforced the Cheyenne's resolve to continue customs and traditions that strengthened their culture. This was especially true of religious customs and ceremonies that became more relevant as the Cheyenne people grew to realize the hopelessness of their condition on the reservation. James A. Cooper, Indian agent at the Cheyenne Reservation in 1890, stated that,

> When General Miles settled these Indians on this so-called reservation and provided them with arms and ammunition the hills and valley were well stocked with buffalo, elk, deer, antelope, etc., thus enabling the Indian to supply his wants by his natural instincts and with little exertion. These resources have gradually changed, until now he would certainly starve if left to them alone for support. However, his instincts and superstitious nature have not changed. The time-honored dance, with its accompanying feast, is just as dear to his savage heart, and the dances are all tinged more or less by some semi-religious superstition.

The agent failed to see the relevance of religious dances to the survival of the Cheyenne people. The Cheyenne participation in the Sun Dance, and by 1890, the Ghost Dance, suggests that they sought renewal of power and Divine intervention to help them again lead an independent life in which they continued their own cultural traditions.

The missionaries realized that they needed to persuade the Cheyenne to abandon customs that reinforced Cheyenne religious culture, especially since it impeded their efforts at conversion. Father Van Der Velden reported that the Cheyenne allowed him to observe traditional ceremonial practices, and believed he witnessed one of the last Sun Dance ceremonies in 1886. Van Der Velden suspected that the Cheyenne invited him to attend their ceremony because they hoped that he "would be most generous at his coming loaded down with tobacco, coffee, sugar, etc., all things they liked to improve their good time." Van Der Velden agreed to attend if he could witness everything about the ceremony. The Cheyenne informed him that he could not see the dance on the morning of the fourth day because he would not like what he saw. This omission caused the priest to refuse the invitation. He later learned that the fourth day was when the young men came forth to prove their manhood in the torture ceremony. During the ceremony, men danced for three days without food or drink. The Cheyenne expected this if participants were to pass the fitness test to qualify as dancers, which to the Cheyenne was equivalent to being soldiers. The longer they danced and the more sacrifice they made, the higher their soldier status. The ultimate test was to be suspended from the center pole by a double bladed knife between the breastbone and the skin.

Some young men who survived the torture ceremony believed that they had special powers that would keep anyone from harming or killing them. Being indestructible was important to young men who were ready to fight for the freedom of their people. This was evident in the summer of 1887 when a Crow Indian by the name of Wraps-up-his-tail participated in the Cheyenne Sun Dance Ceremony. During the dance, he demonstrated his courage by surviving the torture ceremony without giving in to the pain. Out of respect for his bravery, the Cheyenne offered him a present of a medicine saber. With his new status, he assumed the name of Swordbearer and took up the profession of a medicine man. In October, 1887, Crow warriors, under the leadership of Swordbearer, provoked hostility with the United States government--they surrounded and fired shots at the Crow Agency buildings.

It was during this incident that Mother Amadeus and five Ursuline Nuns arrived at Crow Agency. Their destination was St. Xavier's Mission on the Crow Reservation, where the sisters intended to establish a school. During the sisters' first night at the agency, warriors circled the buildings, especially the agent's house, firing their guns at the windows. The agent sent the police to arrest the instigators, but Swordbearer evaded the police. Regardless of the hostility, the sisters opened their mission school shortly after arriving at St. Xavier's in early October. The school, however, closed within a few days because of the excitement generated by Swordbearer, who continued to gain authority among his people.

Girls' school.St. Francis Xavier Mission, 1895. Courtesy of Marquette University, Milwaukee.

The United States government interpreted the actions of Sword-bearer and his followers as an act of war. The army assembled fifteen companies of soldiers at the Crow agency to handle the hostility. They also moved in mountain Howitzers for use by the troops. The army demanded that those who shot at the agency surrender within a certain time period. The Crows did not surrender. The commanding officer sent soldiers to apprehend these warriors. A skirmish followed, and men on both sides were killed. The Crows retreated into the hill country, but government troops wounded Swordbearer during the encounter. When some of his followers saw that he could be wounded like any of them, they realized that his claim of invincibility was false. The Crow incident finally ended when a Crow policeman killed Swordbearer. Regardless of the outcome of the incident, the people did not altogether lose faith in Swordbearer's messiah persona, only his ability to interpret correctly his sacred visions and to direct his power. Swordbearer represented new hope for many Crow people. The incident on the Crow reservation was indicative of the general unrest and dissatisfaction Native Americans had with reservation life.

Mother Amadeus, however, was not alarmed by the Crow hostility. During her stay at the mission, the mother superior did not believe that any of the sisters were in danger. At the time of the unrest she reported that "Large bands of Crows come daily to the fathers and ask their council through the troublesome times." She thought it was ironic that the army brought troops in to protect the "Protestant Agency" and "yet next Monday two of the fathers, myself and an Indian guide will ride right through their country eastward over the mountains in an open wagon over a hundred miles to St. Labre Mission." She attributed their safety to the "influence that our holy religion has already gained on these savages of the mountains."

It was also in 1887 that the Cheyenne allowed Van Der Velden to witness the religious exercise accompanying the Sweathouse Ceremony. The Cheyenne employed the sweathouse, or sweatlodge, with various ceremonies where the participants "took a sweat" before or during the rite. An important aspect of the ceremony was the placement of a bull buffalo skull in front of the sweatlodge by the participant before he went inside. When the person left the lodge, he took his pipe and lifted it up to pray to the God who lives in the sky, asking the deity to keep sufficient buffalo on earth for the Cheyenne to eat. The participant then smoked his pipe in honor of the buffalo skull. By so doing, the Cheyenne believed that the skull would be transformed into a live buffalo.

It was during a Sweathouse Ceremony that White Bull, whom Van Der Velden called "theologian of the tribe," received a message from the spirits that explained to the Cheyenne their dire circumstances. The message was a comingling of Christian and Cheyenne beliefs. White Bull told Van Der Velden,

> The white man is so bad, Blackrobe. God came to the Indians and also to the whites. The former received him with reverence and love; He gave them buffaloes and reindeer in abundance and they were very happy. The whites on the contrary took Him and crucified Him. Seeing that the Pale Faces were so bad. The Great Spirit left the earth never to return, and fixed his abode in heaven. On account of this the Indians who are now unhappy, deprived of game, and their lands are conquered by the white man, who plunders and steals everything, and strive to exterminate the Indian.

The priest further explained White Bulls' vision, "The Great Spirit had visited him [White Bull] during four days and four nights and then had spoken much over the [need] to uproot and destroy the entire white race." Van Der Velden concluded that "hatred for the white is deeply rooted in White Bull."

White Bull's vision was most likely inspired by information he received on a new religious practice among the Plains Indians called the Ghost Dance. The primary function of the Ghost Dance was to bring forth a prophet who could deliver Native American people from hopelessness and despair. The practice of the Ghost Dance is characteristic of what anthropologists call revitalization movements. Revitalization occurs when people attempt to eliminate stress brought on when a society is threatened with cultural destruction. Native Americans, in particular, sought cultural regeneration through the help of an Indian prophet. The prophet usually appeared when an Indian society was in danger of decay or disintegration because of stronger more dominant cultural influences. In all such revitalization movements, prophets carried similar messages. "They taught that the Indians were the chosen people of the Great Spirit and that through a cataclysm the whites and all non-believing Indians would sink away, the earth would be renewed, and the Indians would live in an earthly paradise."

In 1890, the Cheyenne demonstrated resistance to white culture by their participation in the Ghost Dance on the Northern Cheyenne Reservation. Those who practiced the Ghost Dance believed their dancing would call the prophet to come again, save the Indian people, and restore their culture to a time when the Plains would be abundant with buffalo and Native Americans would no longer be hungry. The people believed the longer they danced the sooner the prophet would come. The dance usually lasted four nights, beginning at sundown and ending the next morning, then commencing again the following night. It was common by the end of the dance for the participants to lose consciousness. It was during this time that the missionaries noticed that the Cheyenne were continually "having their Holy Dances" and were openly rebellious. The agent also noticed that the people held dances that lasted for six days and nights. Van Der Velden held little authority among the Cheyenne and, therefore, could not influence the people to abandon their religious dances. Many nights or early mornings the priest witnessed the Cheyenne coming home from their night dances and noticed that they were "drunk with excitement." The Cheyenne showed their malice toward the missionaries by throwing stones at their buildings, hitting the doors and walls. This would happen night after night until the sisters at the mission looked to the priest to put a stop to it. Van Der Velden commented "What can I do? I cannot fight the whole tribe. Please remember we have not yet authority amongst them, first we must establish it by proving we are here for their own good to bring them to heaven."

The missionaries believed that the continuation of Cheyenne dances was a disruptive influence at the boarding school and caused low attendance. Evidently when the children heard the "beating of the drum" and saw the dancers "painted from head to foot and trimmed up with sleigh bells," they left the school to join their parents at the dance house. Van Der Velden wrote to the Commissioner of Indian Affairs of his concern that the practice of traditional dances was a bad influence on boarding school students. The priest suggested that the commissioner instruct the Cheyenne agent to prohibit traditional celebrations. Van Der Velden also informed the Commissioner that the Cheyenne built their dance house with lumber given to them by the agent, which the government intended to be used as flooring and roofing for Cheyenne homes. The missionaries believed that the dance house also served as a place where the Cheyenne people could plot against the missionaries and the government. Van Der Velden commented to the commissioner that the Cheyenne people met at the dance house to "lay their plans, there they decided to break up our school thinking, thereby, to displease the Agent." Despite how Van Der Velden perceived the intentions of the Cheyenne people, he believed that allowing them to continue their traditional life was counter productive to the "civilization" program initiated by the missionaries and the federal government.

The Cheyenne agent viewed the continuation of ceremonial dances differently. He reported that the practice of traditional ceremonies brought the Cheyenne people into direct confrontation with ranchers in the Tongue River valley; it was his opinion that the Cheyenne killed ranchers' livestock for religious purposes because they needed a generous supply of food to sustain dance participants during their long ceremonies. The agent reported "rations were meager; cattle plenty. It became the religious duty of a few to supply meat for the many, that the dance might not cease and thus displease the Great Spirit. Portions of many carcasses of beeves were found on and off the reservation. Naturally there became a strained relation between the rancher and Indian."

Problems involving the Cheyenne people and ranchers along the Tongue River caught the attention of those who traveled or lived in the Tongue River vicinity. George Bird Grinnell, ethnologist and frequent visitor to the Northern Cheyenne Reservation in the 1890s, offered, perhaps, a more accurate explanation of why the Cheyenne were killing range cattle. He noted that "On the Train McPileher, First Cavalry stationed at Custer told me that the whole cause of the troubles of the Cheyenne agency at Rosebud this spring or summer was due to the fact that the Indians were starving. The supplies issued them by the gov't were insufficient to support life, and they killed some of the beef which is always grazing on their reservation."

It was during this time that the murder of several whites sent a general alarm through the white community. In May 1890, a cowboy named Bob Ferguson was found murdered. Ferguson worked for a rancher in the Tongue River area. His employer declared him missing when Ferguson failed to return to the ranch after a routine search for stray horses. For over a week, settlers in the area searched for the missing ranch hand. They eventually found Ferguson "wrapped in blankets, buried with his saddle in the side of a hill; nearby lay his horse, dead, having been shot, as did also part of the carcass of a steer." From this evidence, the authorities concluded that Ferguson must have caught the Cheyenne butchering a steer that did not belong to them. Alarmed, the Cheyenne killed and buried the cowboy. The authorities arrested five Cheyenne, but the evidence was circumstantial and they eventually set the accused free.

On September 13, 1890, whites also accused the Cheyenne of killing a Lame Deer man by the name of Hugh Doyle. Evidently, Doyle was rounding up stray horses for a rancher by the name of McGaffney. The Weekly *Yellowstone Journal* reported that McGaffney's ranch was "located on the so called Cheyenne Reservation." The *Journal* continued by stating that "with the news of the discharge of Ferguson's murders coming simultaneously with the murder of Hugh Doyle, the forbearance of the settlers will be tried to the utmost, a serious outcome will surprise nobody."

Until the federal government settled the dispute between Indian and white over the boundaries of the Cheyenne Reservation, hostility continued. In their efforts to move the Northern Cheyenne Reservation from the Tongue River, stockgrowers and residents of Miles City wrote numerous letters and memorials to territorial and federal officials accusing the Cheyenne of slaughtering ranchers' stock and disrupting the movement of cattle through the area. White settlers believed that the best solution to the "Indian problem" was to remove the Cheyenne from the Tongue River to the Pine Ridge Reservation in South Dakota. Senator Frank Pettigrew of South Dakota opposed this plan because there was no land left at Pine Ridge for the Cheyenne; therefore, they could never become self-supporting. The Land Commissioner of Montana fought for Cheyenne removal on the pretense that the Tongue River Reservation could not be irrigated. It was also his opinion that "all that Montanans cared about was to have the Cheyenne removed to some other point or place under military surveillance." One obstacle to settling the question of land ownership along the Tongue River was the lack of federal policy for the Northern Cheyenne Reservation. Without a coherent policy, the Interior Secretary and Indian Commissioner could not evaluate the land rights of the Northern Cheyenne or the stockgrowers.

The Catholic missionaries experienced some of the hostility the Cheyenne held toward the federal government and the ranchers. For the most part, the Cheyenne people rejected Catholic doctrine and the dictates of white culture. So much so that when Father Cataldo visited St. Labre's Mission in 1892, he proclaimed that the missionaries wasted their labor on the Northern Cheyenne. Cataldo sent the missionaries to St. Xavier's Mission on the Crow Reservation, where he believed their work would be more fruitful. Van Der Velden returned to St. Labre's Mission for a five week visit. During his stay, he concluded that the Cheyenne were now more receptive to Catholic instruction. He wrote,

> They began to miss us and came up every evening in good numbers for prayers; a few also have come to confession and communion. Although they are hard to get along with, still I like to work among them. When we left they, for the first time manifested their displeasure. This was a good sign and there is still hope that St. Labre's must not be abandoned completely.

Perhaps in light of Van Der Velden's optimism that the Cheyenne could be Christianized, Father Cataldo sent the missionaries back to St. Labre's Mission in March, 1893. For the next several years, the missionaries reported that there were no major incidents to provoke renewed hostility. During this peaceful interlude, they busied themselves with building a church at the mission for the Cheyenne people.The peace at the Cheyenne mission was broken in 1897 when unrest between Indian and white mounted in the wake of another murder. In that year ranchers found sheepherder John Hoover's body several miles from the reservation. The ranchers assumed that the Cheyenne had murdered Hoover, because next to his body lay a beef carcass. Supposedly, Hoover had caught the Cheyenne in the act of killing white owned beef. Outraged ranchers took up arms and vowed revenge. The threat of impending trouble alarmed white settlers and the Indian community. While Cheyenne women and children escaped to the hills, their men armed themselves against imminent danger. The Cheyenne man who shot Hoover hid in the hills until found by his own people. He surrendered to them. The authorities eventually tried and convicted him for murder in Miles City and confined him to the prison at Deer Lodge. The Hoover incident provided the ranchers with another opportunity to warn federal officials of the "Indian problem" in the Tongue River vicinity.

It concerned Mother Amadeus that her sisters were at the mission during this time of unrest. A chronicler at St. Peter's wrote:

> The Cheyenne were on the warpath and Mother was most anxious to leave to go to our Nuns there but was detained by Father Bandini's violent opposition to her departure, and the heavy and constant rains. Badger, brother of Lucia, one of our girls at the Cheyenne Mission, murdered Hoover, a sheepherder at Barringer's ranch. The whites demanded his surrender, which was finally done by White Bull, the chief. In the interval, much excitement prevailed and all the women were removed from the Reservation. Mother M. Angela telegraphed to Mother that our Nuns were in great danger and Mother spent the interval in great anxiety.

Van Der Velden believed that the white community resented his efforts to defend the Cheyenne people. In 1897, the priest claimed that some whites were trying to kill him because he took the side of the Cheyenne. He wrote to his brother that,

> The whites were after my life, my death was resolved upon, and only because I took the part of the Indians. In one day I received three warnings from friendly persons, to leave the Indians over to themselves because if I would not I would not see the mission again. The third warning had its effect, for the entire plan of the whites was shown to me. An old drunkard had agreed to shoot me through the head.

Van Der Velden learned of the murder plot while visiting the Cheyenne agency at Lame Deer. Perceiving that his life was in danger, he took refuge at the Cheyenne mission. The priest heard next that there was a plan to link him with the death of the sheepherder. Evidently, Van Der Velden believed that the prosecuting attorney in Miles City sided with the ranchers against the Cheyenne and issued a subpoena for the priest to testify at the trial of those accused of the sheepherder's murder. According to the Jesuit, the prosecuting attorney, "in order to satisfy his clients, endeavored to drag me into the affair under the pretense I knew all about it. The papers were already at the undersheriff." Van Der Velden agreed to testify; however, he suspected that he would be linked to the murder and placed in prison. The Jesuit agreed to appear at the trial, indicating that he would stop off in Miles City while traveling to Spokane. According to the priest, he intended to "throw them off track," while he retreated to the Catholic mission on the Crow Reservation. Complicating Van Der Velden's escape from the authorities was the deterioration of his health. In 1893, the priest experienced a burst artery that he believed was caused from "overwork, irregular and not sufficient food, most of all lack of sufficient night rest." Van Der Velden often complained in letters to his family of the difficult nature of his work at St. Labre's Mission. His biggest complaint was the lack of rest, because day and night he tended to the needs of the Cheyenne people. He wrote to his brother that "this evening I was called to a sick person. The entire evening gone. Now it is deep in the night. My eyes are closing. Shall I go to sleep? I would like too. See here the last four nights: Quarter to two, two, half past two o'clock I went to bed. Throughout the day not a minute for rest." Before leaving St. Labre's Mission in 1897, the missionaries found Van Der Velden unconscious several times. His condition worsened at the Crow mission. The Jesuits took Van Der Velden to the hospital at Camp Custer, where doctors diagnosed his ailment as "wandering typhus." He spent the first fourteen days at the hospital in a coma. The disease caused heart and kidney damage, plus a loss of memory. He convalesced in Spokane for two months. From the time he recovered to his death in 1925, the Jesuits gave Van Der Velden missionary assignments that were less arduous than those at the Cheyenne mission.

The renewed outbreak of the Ghost Dance and the incidence of Cheyenne warfare caused the Jesuits to abandon permanently their work at St. Labre's Mission in 1897. In 1898, the government sent a representative to investigate the dispute between Indian and white over the reservation boundaries. After buying out the settlers who owned land on or near the reservation, the government issued an executive order on March 19, 1900 that set the new boundary lines. The survey increased the reservation to over 460,000 acres. Also after 1900, the federal government amended their agricultural program for the Northern Cheyenne Reservation. Instead of emphasizing farming, the government supplied the reservation with cattle and equipment for stockraising.

When the missionaries first went to St. Labre's Mission, they believed that they could successfully weaken and ultimately eliminate Native American culture by replacing it with Roman Catholicism. As Catholic missionaries, their function was to save Indian souls and show them the way to heaven. They realized little success among the Cheyenne because their culture sustained them better in dire poverty than did Christian beliefs. The Ursuline sisters reflected this failure in their comments at Van Der Velden's departure and showed them the way to heaven.

> The last wagonload of freight rolled off drawn by Mr. Ed Yeager and then Fathers Van Der Velden and Van Der Pol drove off in a buggy. Father Van Der Velden had labored here 12 years and rode off today broken in heart and health, begging God to call him soon to Himself.

Van Der Velden did realize that the work to "civilize" the Cheyenne people would continue into the twentieth century. Shortly before he left the mission in 1897, he observed that "all hope was to be found in the school." The experience of his tenure at St. Labre's Mission convinced him that the adult Indian could not be converted to Christianity. Father Van Der Velden surmised that the "Low foundation upon which their code of morality was build [sic], and the next to impossible overthrowing of their pagan customs were insurmountable obstacles." He did believe, however, that there was a chance to civilize the next generation if they attended the boarding school where there was little contact with Indian parents and Indian culture.

After Father Van Der Velden left St. Labre's Mission in 1897, The Catholics sent men from other orders to continue acculturation programs. The Ursuline Nuns continued to educate Cheyenne children no matter how difficult the environment or how small the school attendance. The Ursulines stayed at St. Labre's Mission until 1932.

Ursuline nuns. St. Mary's Mission, Akulurak, Alaska. Courtesy of Jesuit Oregon Province Archive, Gonzaga University, Spokane.

6

THE TRAIL TO ALASKA

By the 1890s, Mother Amadeus considered her missionary work in Montana finished. She had established eight schools on reservations and in towns in eastern Montana and a kindergarten at St. Ignatius Mission on the Flathead Reservation in western Montana. In 1898, she wrote Father Pascal Tosi, Vice Superior of the Jesuits in Alaska, seeking permission for the Ursulines to undertake missionary work in the far north. She informed the father that, "Missionary life in Montana has nearly come to a close so we must look for new fields for Indian work." In her letter, she pleaded with him to accept the Ursulines as Alaskan missionaries. She assured Tosi that the sisters would assume all expenses and that they could endure the hardships. She wrote:

> The poverty of the Alaska missions does in no way dis-
> courage us. We are ready, with the help of God, for every
> sacrifice, so I beg of you, Father, not to be afraid to take
> us with you this summer for Nulato or, preferably, for
> Kotzebue Sound [In the Arctic Circle]. We can live on
> what the natives live on and in the same kind of houses
> or dwellings.

Mother Amadeus was aware that, in order for her to establish a branch of the Ursuline foundation in the far north, she would need permission from the Jesuits, with many of whom she had an acrimonious relationship. As Superior of the Montana Ursulines, it was her responsibility to maintain the integrity of her order while at the same time working with the Jesuits, who were the final authority on matters pertaining to the operation of the missions. Mother Amadeus knew she would need Bishop Brondel's permission to expand the Ursuline foundation out of Montana. She was aware that getting permission could be difficult because she and Bishop Brondel didn't always agree on matters pertaining to mission life. The mother superior went over Brondel's head to Father Tosi. She was anxious for Tosi's acceptance so that she could then inform Brondel that Tosi wanted the Ursulines. Brondel, however, did not grant Mother Amadeus' request to leave Montana. It could be assumed that the bishop was reluctant to lose sisters from Montana missions. Mother Amadeus thought otherwise. She wrote to Tosi that "I exceedingly regret to say that I did not yet obtain the bishop's consent to go to Alaska. By the way his Lordship spoke, I think he does not like the application for the Ursulines to go to Alaska to come from me." Mother Amadeus was not one to be discouraged by formidable obstacles. In 1900, when Pope Leo XIII invited Ursulines from all over the world to gather in Rome to vote on uniting the different Ursuline houses into one political body. Mother Amadeus seized the opportunity to lobby for an expansion of her foundation to Alaska. She traveled, then, to the Holy City for two reasons: to attend the conference and to obtain permission to move to Alaska. While at the conference, Mother Amadeus worked to unite all Ursuline communities into one Union, she cast eight votes for her Montana missions in support of a united congregation. Union membership meant that funds from all houses would be distributed to the most needy convents. Montana convents came under this category. Most Ursulines were in support of such a merger and the issue passed. After the vote, the next order of business was to elect union officers. The sisters elected Mother St. Julian as General of the Ursuline Union. The Ursuline Union was a powerful political body, much like the Jesuit organization, and it allowed the sisters an authoritative voice in missionary activities. So, while in Rome, Mother Amadeus asked the newly elected general of the Ursuline Union for permission to expand Ursuline mission work to Alaska. Mother St. Julian granted Mother Amadeus permission and appointed the Montana Ursulines to supervise the establishment of Alaskan mission schools. Alaska was one of the last frontiers for missionary work among Native people. Undoubtedly, the adventure of starting over in unmarked territory was an exciting challenge for Mother Amadeus. There were, however, many dangers and hardships awaiting the sisters.

Roman Catholic missionary work in Alaska began in 1870 when Father Emile Petitot explored the Upper Yukon Basin. But, the Anglican church had already established a mission in this area; Father Petitot decided not to compete with the Anglicans. Reverend Charles J. Seghers, Archbishop of Oregon Providence, was the next to mount an exploratory trip to investigate establishing Catholic missions. Since the Anglicans had the Upper Yukon Basin, Seghers, traveled to the Pacific Coastal region in 1878. He found the Russian church well entrenched in this area. A few years later Seghers tried again; this time he concentrated on the Alaskan interior along the Middle Yukon River around Nulato. He found the region unoccupied by any religious foundation, but it was not until 1886 that he traveled to the region to begin work on establishing a Catholic presence among the Native people around Nulato. Seghers, however, never lived to see the fulfillment of his dream. His story serves as an example of some of the dangers the sisters faced in frontier Alaska.

Seghers traveled to the Middle Yukon Basin in 1886 with Fathers P. Tosi and A. Robaut and Francis Fuller, a stranger who volunteered to guide the Archbishop on his journeys. Fuller displayed some odd characteristics, and by the time the party reached Juneau, Father Tosi tried to convince Fuller that he should take the return boat to Vancouver. Fuller claimed great devotion to Seghers and convinced the trio that he should continue to be their guide. Tosi had his doubts about Fuller; something about the guide troubled the priest. At any rate, the party made their way to Skagway and over Chilcoot Pass to the headwaters of the Yukon. It was at this point that the four decided to separate; Fathers Tosi and Robaut continued to the upper reaches of the Yukon to explore Indian settlements along the river; Seghers and Fuller traveled down river as far as Nulato. The plan was to reunite again at St. Michael's.

The Archbishop and Fuller traveled down the Yukon for a thousand miles, a trip that lasted almost one month. When they reached Nukloroyet, the Archbishop decided to rest for a couple of days. While at Nukloroyet, Seghers met a merchant named Walker. As the story goes, Walker disliked anything religious. So much so that he tried to discourage the Catholics from settling along the Yukon. Walker influenced Fuller to try and stop Catholic immigration. According to Segher's diary, which was found later, Fuller's attitude toward Segher became hostile and antagonistic. Segher thought it better if he continued his travels without the guide. Segher, then, had to wait six weeks for the ice to become strong enough to support a sled and a team of dogs in order to continue the trip Nulato. By the time the Archbishop was ready to travel, Fuller demanded that he travel with Seghers. The two set off and within a week reached a small post run by a Russian named Korkorin. Korkorin was quick to see that Fuller was trouble. He thought it wise to escort Seghers to Nulato; he sent two Natives guides. After a week Seghers and company came to an old fishing hut, where they spent the night protected from the winter cold. For reasons not clear to anyone at the time or since, Fuller finally lost control and shot Seghers through the heart as he was getting up to prepare for the last day of travel.

The Segher incident was well known throughout the Pacific Northwest and certainly by the Catholic sisters who fought to get permission to establish themselves at one or more of the missions established by the Jesuits. The dangers inherent to the frontier did not phase the sisters. Their attitude seemed to be that they really were only serving God if they were deprived of the comforts hearth and home. This was certainly true in Alaska.

Fathers Tosi and Robaut discovered the death of the Archbishop the following summer. After collecting the details from the guides sent by the Russian and listening to Fuller's demented explanation, they reported the incident to Vancouver and Rome. It is not clear what action was taken against Fuller for the murder of Archbishop Segher. Tosi and Robaut continued their search for a mission site and in 1888 opened Holy Cross Mission in the lower Yukon region about twenty-five miles below Anvik, opposite Koserefski. Father Tosi invited the Sisters of St. Anne from Lachine, Quebec, to establish a school at the mission.

Mother Amadeus watched as one religious order after another received assignments in Alaska. Finally, on August 13th, 1905, she and two of her Montana sisters, a French exile who had served for two years in Montana and a sister who served twelve years at Ursuline missions, booked passage on the *S.S. Senator* bound for St. Michael's in Alaska.

The sisters' destination was St. Mary's Mission at the remote outpost of Akulurak, a native village in the Yukon Delta.

What the Ursulines found at Akulurak was a wind-swept plain of moss-covered tundra on the Bering Sea. To most the remote outpost would have seemed barren and desolate. But, the missionaries thought the silence of the region to be contemplative. As one Jesuit described it, it was "a kind of solemn religious silence like that of a great cathedral when the worshipers are gone; no sound, no noise of any kind, not even the chirping of a cricket; the very birds, besides being extremely rare here, do not sing." In the quietude of this coastal land stood two log structures, one for the fathers, and the other for the Ursulines and twenty-six Inuit children. The sisters' log convent was 24x26 in dimension. In this space there was a chapel, kitchen, classroom, and a dormitory for the children under the eaves. A unique characteristic of the convent was that at night the sisters could see the stars through the cracks in the roof.

The sisters' work at St. Mary's was, perhaps, more difficult than at missions in Montana. The hardships were certainly more challenging. The cold environment made the sisters' work more difficult than at missions

First Ursuline convent, St. Mary's Mission, Akulurak, Alaska, 1904. Courtesy of Jesuit Oregon Province Archive, Gonzaga University, Spokane.

farther south. In the winter the average temperature was around five below zero but often as low as forty below. In the summer it could be in the eighties and nineties, but summer was only a couple of months; the snow began in September and usually lasted through May. The sisters depended on the climate as well. In the long winter months they were able to move about by malamute-pulled sleds, and in the summer by boat through the bough and swamp that surrounded the mission. In this inhospitable climate, the sisters took care of the children's needs, mending and washing the clothes for an average of eighty-five children. Washing the clothes was certainly one of the most undesirable chores. In the winter months the laundry was dark and cold, and after washing clothes they had to be dried out of doors in the cold arctic wind. When the sisters weren't seeing to the duties of daily life(besides laundry, they baked an endless number of loaves of bread each day and dried 22,000 fish each year) the sisters met with the children to teach them catechism and the English language. The children were also taught skills of survival; along with homemaking skills the girls learned how to skin animals. The boys learned to hunt, trap, and fish. There didn't seem to be the same emphasis given to changing the culture of Eskimo children as there was of the Native children at missions in Montana.

Mother Amadeus did not stay in Alaska. She was only given permission to establish the Ursulines. Her primary responsibility was to supervise the Montana foundations. But, in 1910, Mother Amadeus returned to Rome for the third meeting of the Ursuline Union. At the meeting, Mother St. Julian appointed Mother Amadeus Provincial of Alaska and gave her permission to engage actively in missionary work. From Rome, Mother Amadeus traveled directly to St. Michael's, a trade center on the Bering Sea. At St. Michael's, she established St. Ursula's-by-the-Sea. A structure made of rough boards and tarpaper was the Ursulines' convent. According to Mother Angela Lincoln, who accompanied Mother Amadeus from Rome, the new convent had its limitations:

> The furious wind tore off the tar paper from the tiny cabin
> that stood out upon the bluff behind the church. The green
> lumber was shrinking so that we could have slipped our
> hands between the boards on those dreadful night when
> our poor walls seemed the strings of some wild Aeolian
> harp upon which the winds kept singing their weird melo-

Ursuline nuns, Yukon River, Alaska. Courtesy of Jesuit Oregon Province
Archives, Gonzaga University, Spokane.

Ursuline nuns drying fish. St. Mary's Mission, Akulurak, Alaska. Courtesy of
Jesuit Oregon Province Archives, Gonzaga University, Spokane.

dies. Often during that first winter, we sat up all night asking God to save us, for we feared we would be dashed into
the Bering as other cabins were. Mother Amadeus had
chosen the coldest corner of the dormitory for herself, and
one of her feet was frozen. It was so cold that we had to
wear our parkees [fur coat, seamless and slipped on over
the head] all night. We could not make a fire for the wind
was so high and the price of coal still higher.

From St. Michael's Mother Amadeus traveled to Valdez, where
Rev. R. J. Crimont, S.J., asked her to establish a school.
Missionary life in Alaska was difficult. The harshness of the climate, the lack of transportation, the inadequate living conditions, and the
loneliness of isolated outposts on the Bering Sea could deprive the sisters
of the strength they needed to educate and Christianize Native children.
Even though living a deprived life was upholding their vows as religious,
Mother Amadeus believed that there should be a home established for the
sisters where they could retreat from their missionary duties in order to enjoy contemplation and isolation from the outside world. In 1914 in Seattle,
Washington, Mother Amadeus established a novitiate, Mount St. Helen's
Place, to prepare women for missionary duty in Alaska and to provide "a
trysting place in a milder climate, where the Alaskan missionaries may
recover every ten years or so, the strength worn by loneliness, cold, and
privation."
Mother Amadeus supervised her Alaskan missions in much the
same manner as she supervised her Montana missions--she traveled from
one mission to another conferring with her nuns and updating facilities.
The supervision of Alaskan missions was, however, more arduous. She
not only had the difficulty of traveling between missions but also between
Seattle and Alaska. Storms often prevented her from reaching her destination, sometimes forcing her to return to Seattle. On one of her visits to the
missions in 1918, Mother Amadeus fell from her berth during a storm. The
fall severely injured the mother superior, the missionaries took her to St.
Michael's to recovered at Ursula-by-the-Sea. During her convalescence,
the convent burned to the ground. They carried Mother Amadeus from the
burning structure and later escorted her to Seattle, where she died November 10, 1919.

7

THE TRAIL TO
THE 21ST CENTURY

Some of the Catholic sisters worked for over fifty years in mission schools and hospitals in Montana. They began their missionary labors with language and cultural barriers and few financial resources with which to educate Native American children. The Sisters of Providence built boarding schools and a hospital at St. Ignatius and St. Patrick's Hospital in Missoula. At one time, mission schools included elementary and secondary programs and a boarding school for orphaned children. As financial resources diminished, the Catholics closed the high school in 1940, and the boarding school during the 1960s. By the 1970s, they had eliminated the seventh and eighth grades from the elementary school. Visiting St. Ignatius in the twentieth-first century, one finds only St. Ignatius Church still actively serving the Flathead people. The only evidence of the four French sisters from Montreal who build schools and a hospital at St. Ignatius is their original log cabin, which is open to tourists, if, by chance, they should stop for gas in the little town of St. Ignatius. And as visitors drive north on highway 93 toward Flathead Lake, they will see the Mission Mountains rising toward the sky. They will pass through towns like Arlee, named for Flathead Chief Arlee, and Ronan named for the Indian Agent who helped the Jesuits and sisters in their building programs. Even the Indian agent's wife has special recognition in a beautiful mountain lake named Lake Mary Ronan.

But, perhaps the biggest tribute to the Sisters of Providence is their hospital in Missoula. Today St. Patrick's Hospital is one of the leading health centers in the Pacific Northwest. From the cabin on the banks of the Clark Fork River, the sisters' one-room convent, school and hospital went through many transformations, growing bigger each time. Today in 2002, St. Patrick's Hospital and Health Science Center is again under construction. The new facility will be six stories high with physician's offices and outpatient services and an underground parking garage.

By 1900, the missionary struggle to convert and educate Native Americans had ended. It was hard to maintain educational programs and facilities after the withdrawal of federal and BCIM funds. The Ursuline Nuns took up the challenge of educating Native American children at St. Ignatius when the Sisters of Providence turned their efforts to providing health care in western Montana. The Ursulines stayed at St. Ignatius Mission until the 1980s. Mother Amadeus and the Ursuline sisters who followed her to Montana and Alaska are buried in the cemetery on the hill behind St. Ignatius Church overlooking the beautiful Mission Mountains.

In all, the Ursuline Nuns established seven mission schools for Native American children and two schools for white girls. Remnants of the old Ursuline laundry are all that remains of St. Peter's Mission near Bird Tail Rock. The schools for boys and girls burned in 1908. At that time the Catholics discontinued the boys' school. In 1912, the Ursulines moved the school for white girls to Great Falls. The city eventually became the center of Ursuline activity in Montana. The school for Native American girls continued at the mission until another fire destroyed their building in 1918. The Ursulines left Holy Family Mission on the Blackfoot Reservation in 1935 when it closed owing to financial difficulties. In the 1930s, the Ursulines also left St. Paul's and St. Xavier's Missions.

Ironically, St. Labre's Mission, where the Catholics encountered so much Native American resistance to educational programs, has the only mission school still operating in the twenty-first century. Today St. Labre's Indian school, located along the banks of the Tongue River in southeastern Montana, serves both the Cheyenne and Crow people. The enrollment at four schools in St. Labre's system is 700 students. The Catholics have established a modern campus with dormitories to house students during the week. On the weekend they are returned to their homes as far as 40 miles away.

SOURCES

Archives

There are several collections containing primary sources that are very important to the study of the Catholic sisters at Indian missions in Montana. The Bureau of Catholic Indian Missions records at Marquette University, Milwaukee, Wisconsin contains correspondence between the Jesuit fathers and Catholic officials at the Bureau concerning the operations of the Montana missions. See, The letters of J. Giorda, S.J., Van Gorp, S.J., L.B.Palladion, S.J., Peter Prondo, S.J., Charles S. Lusk, D. Shanahan and Father Brouillet, S.J. in the Montana Collection, St. Ignatius Mission. And, Joseph Cataldo, S.J., Montana Collection, St. Peters' Mission.

The papers and letters of the Jesuits and sisters at Jesuit missions in Montana are also housed in the Oregon Province Archives of the Society of Jesus, at the Ralph E. and Helen Higgins Foley Center, Gonzaga University, Spokane, Washington. The bulk of the archive collection is on microfilm and available through inter-library loan. The Foley Library also has historical files that offer further information. Important to this study is the Ursuline file and the Katharine Drexel file.

Besides the Jesuit Archives, Convent Archives have information on the sisters. The sisters who traveled to St. Ignatius in 1864 were from the Sisters of Charity of Providence convent in Montreal, Canada. From their archive I was able to obtain, *The Institute of Providence, Traite Elementaire De Matiere Medicale et Guide Practique des Soeurs de Charte* and *Necrologies Des Filles De La Charite'*.

From the Sister of Providence in Spokane, Washington, a valuable source that details important events in the first couple of years at St. Ignatius; The *Chonicles, 1864-1873.*

Information on the Ursulines can be found in the following convent archives.

Ursuline Convent, Toledo, Ohio

Professional Records; Sarah Threse Dunne, Christine Seibert, Louise Abair, Louise Carabin, Bridget McFarland and Suzanne Meilink.

"Prospectus, Ursuline Convent of the Sacred Heart of Jesus."

Letters
Sister St. Francis to Mother Stanislaus, 10 January 1884.
Mother Amadeus to Mother Stanislaus, 18 January 1884.
Sister St. Angela to Mother Stanislaus, 27 January 1884.
Sister St. Francis to Mother Stanislaus, 28 January 1884.
Mother Amadeus to Mother Stanislaus, 29 January 1884.
Sister Sacred Heart to Mother Stanislaus, 2 February 1884.
Sister St. Francis to Mother Stanislaus, 30 March 1884
Sister Ignatius to Mother Stanislaus, 27 April 1884
Mother Amadeus to Mother Stanislaus, 14 July 1884.
Mother Amadeus to Mother Stanislaus, 18 August 1884.
Mother Amadeus to Mother Stanislaus, 10 October 1884.
Mother Amadeus to Mother Stanislaus, 11 November 1884.
Sister Sacred Heart to Mother Stanislaus, 16 November 1884.
Sister Mary of the Angels to Mother Stanislaus, 28 May 1885.
Mother Amadeus to Mother Stanislaus, 5 September 1887.
Mother Amadeus to Mother Stanislaus, 7 October 1887.
Mother Amadeus to Mother Stanislaus, 10 March 1888.
School Sisters of St. Francis Convent. Milwaukee, Wisconsin.
Maria Eustella, O.S.F., "Sand, Sage, and Struggle."
Mother Amadeus to Mother Stanislaus, 18 January 1884.
Mother Amadeus to Mother Stanislaus, 29 January 1884.

Ursuline Convent. Great Falls, Montana.
"Religious Orders of Women," *Sponsa Regis.*
"Mustard Seed in Montana"
"Ursulines in Montana"
"Unidentified publication"

Ursuline Convent. St. Martin, Ohio.
Professional Records, Florence Lincoln, 22 November 1881.

State and Governmental archives contain the following:

Montana Historical Society. Helena, Montana.
Small Collection:
Pierre Jean De Smet to Reverend Mother Superior, 29 November 1863.
Peter Prondo, S.J., "History of St. Xavier's Mission."

Montana Collection. Mansfield Library. University of Montana. Missoula, Montana.

C. E. Schaeffer, An Acculturation Study of the Indians of the Flathead Reservation of Western Montana, 1935.

Government Documents:
Annual Report of the Commissioner of Indian Affairs to the Secretary of the Interior for the Year 1857. Washington: U.S. Government Printing Office, 1957.

Annual Report of the Commissioner of Indian Affairs to the Secretary of the Interior for the Year 1874. Washington: U.S. Government Printing Office, 1974.

Annual Report of the Commissioner of Indian Affairs to the Secretary of the Interior for the Year 1888. Washington: U.S. Government Printing Office, 1888.

Annual Report of the Commissioner of Indian Affairs to the Secretary of the Interior for the Year 1890. Washington: U.S. Government Printing Office, 1890.

Indian Appropriations. Congressional Record, XV. 1884. Washington: Government Printing Office.

Indian Appropriations. Congressional Record, XXII, 1891. Washington: Government Printing Office.

Kappler, Charles J. *Laws and Treaties*, Vol. II. Washington: Government Printing Office, 1904.

Mooney, James. *The Ghost Dance Religion and the Sioux Outbreak.*
Fourteenth Annual Report of the Bureau of Ethnology to the Secretary of the Smithsonian Institutions. Washington: Government Printing Office, 1896.

Report on Population of the United States at the Eleventh Census: 1890, Part II. Washington: Government Printing Office, 1890.

U.S. Congress. *Indian Appropriations.* 48th Cong., 1st sess., 1884. *Congressional Record* Vol. 15.

U.S. Congress. *Indian Appropriations.* 51st Cong., 1st sess., 1890.*Congressional Record* Vol. 21.

U.S. Congress. *House Executive Document 169*, 43rd Cong., 1st sess., 1874.

U.S. Congress. *House Executive Document 107*, 53rd Cong., 3rd sess., 1894.

U.S. Congress. *Senate Document 17*, 36th Cong., 1st sess., 1864.

INDEX

A

Amadeus, Mother 4, 41, 42, 44, 45, 46, 47, 48, 49, 50, 52, 54, 56, 59, 60, 61,
    63, 65, 70, 71, 80, 83, 84, 90, 95, 96, 97, 98, 100, 102, 104
Arapaho Indians 55, 67
Arkansas River 66
Arlee, MT 103
Assiniboine Indians 48, 55
Atsina Indians 55

B

Bandini, Rev. Joseph 33
Barcelo, Peter, S.J. 41, 70, 71
BCIM 30, 32, 33, 34, 35, 38, 54, 59, 60, 61, 104
Bird Tail Rock 49, 104
Bitterroot Valley 34
Blackfoot 4, 35, 41, 48, 49, 50, 54, 55, 60, 61, 63, 104
Blackfoot Reservation 104
Blanchet, Rev. Norbet 6
Blood Indians 61
Board of Indian Commissioners 30
Bourget, Bishop 6
Brondel, Bishop John B. 42, 44, 45, 46, 47, 48, 49, 52, 65, 70, 71, 81, 96
Brouillet, Rev. 35
Bureau of Catholic Indian Missions 30. *See* BCIM
Bureau of Indian Affairs 30, 31, 33, 54

C

Carlisle Indian School 57, 58
Caron, Mother Emily 16, 25, 26
Carter, Senator Thomas H. 61
Cascade, MT 49, 52
Cataldo, Fr. Joseph 36, 38, 54, 60, 89, 90
Cheyenne Indians 4, 41, 42, 50, 63, 65, 66, 67, 68, 69, 70, 71, 72, 73, 74, 75,
    76, 77, 78, 80, 81, 82, 83, 85, 86, 87, 88, 89, 90, 91, 92, 93, 104
Cheyenne Reservation 4, 68
Chief Arlee 34, 103
Chief Michelle 34
Chief White Calf 60
Chilcoot Pass 97
Cleveland, Grover 55
Coeur d'Alene 12
Columbia River 11

S

Swordbearer 83, 84

T

Taho Agency 31
Toledo, Ohio 4
Tongue River 66, 67, 68, 71, 87, 88, 89, 90, 104
Tongue River Valley 66
Tosi, Pascal, S.J. 95, 96, 97, 98
Two Medicine Creek 60
Two Medicine River 63

U

University of Victoria 7, 24
Ursuline 4, 5, 7, 8, 36, 37, 41, 42, 46, 47, 48, 49, 54, 66, 76, 83, 92, 93, 95, 96,
        98, 100, 104, vii, viii
Ursulines 4, 8, 36, 37, 39, 41, 42, 44, 46, 47, 48, 49, 50, 52, 54, 56, 59, 60, 61,
        62, 63, 65, 66, 68, 69, 77, 81, 93, 95, 96, 99, 100, 104, vii
Ursuline Congregation of Paris 5

V

Valdez, AK 102
Van Der Velden, Aloysius, S.J. 65, 66, 74, 75, 76, 77, 80, 81, 82, 83, 85, 86, 87,
        89, 91, 92, 93
Van Gorp, Leopold, S.J. 32
Vest, Senator George G. 29

W

Walker 97
Walla Walla, WA 11, 16
White Bull 70, 85, 86
Willamette River 6
Wraps-up-his-tail 83

Y

Yeager, Ed 92
Yellow Stocking 70
Yoakum, George 71